Supernatural Marriage

Dan Wilson, M.D.

Supernatural Marriage

THE JOY OF SPIRIT-LED INTIMACY

Dan Wilson, M.D.

Published by XP Publishing
A department of Christian Services Association
P.O. Box 1017
Maricopa, Arizona 85139
www.XPpublishing.com

ISBN-13: 978-1-936101-13-9
ISBN-10: 1-936101-13-0

Printed in Canada. For Worldwide Distribution.

Endorsements

The men of Issachar from 1 Chronicles 12:32 understood the times and knew what to do. In the times in which we are living today, the infrastructure of world society is deteriorating due to the onslaught of the enemy against covenant relationships in this hour. Dan Wilson's timely book *Supernatural Marriage* will inspire you to seek and find improved intimacy with your spouse by allowing the Holy Spirit to draw you together towards complete oneness in Him.

DR. ROBERT STEARNS
Executive Director
Eagles' Wings Ministries, Clarence, New York

Dan Wilson draws couples into a new realm of union that reflects the oneness believers will experience eternally with their Bridegroom Jesus. Let your marriage be supernaturally transformed through the pages of this book by our covenant-keeping God.

CHÉ AHN
Senior Pastor, Harvest Rock Church
President and Founder, Harvest International Ministry

Healthy marriages and families are the backbone of a stable and prosperous nation. Today, more than ever, we need good, solid encouragement and instruction on how to enjoy a marriage that is like heaven on earth. Dr. Dan Wilson's book, *Supernatural Marriage*, will both refresh and empower your faith to lay hold of the fullness of all God has for you in marriage. No matter where you have walked, what you have gone through, there are keys contained in this book that will enable you to embrace new beginnings.

PATRICIA KING
President of XPmedia

Dan Wilson brilliantly weaves together the story of his supernatural encounters with God and how they have transformed both his life and his marriage. In *Supernatural Marriage*, you will get an inside look into the process of how God opened Dan's heart to receive this truth, the lessons he had to learn along the way – particularly that of lordship – and how living in God's supernatural presence has brought great benefits and blessings into his marriage. This is a timely and needed message for marriages in the church today. Once again, God chooses to touch every person in the body of Christ – the little ol' me's – with His presence and for His glory. Dan is certainly no exception.

RANDY CLARK
Founder and President
Global Awakening

What a story and testimony of a walk with God in marriage! This is what God intended when He created marriage for our good and welfare. As in all of life, we cannot live supernaturally without God in our affairs. We were not meant to love and live outside of God and His amazing grace. In a day when so many marriages are on the rocks, such a book is really needed to be able to appropriate the truths and The Truth that make such a marriage possible. Indeed a cord of three strands is the secret of such a time together! May our Lord revive holy marriage in our churches and homes.

PETER LORD
Pastor, speaker, author of *The 2959 Plan*
and many more resources

Long before Dan put pen to paper, those of us who have been blessed to know Dan and Linda have seen the unfolding of the concepts of this book. Their marriage has been godly, beautiful, and deep for decades. How incredible to see the transformation of a truly exemplary marriage into a supernatural marriage! The increased depth of oneness, passion, power, and joy in the Holy Spirit are invitingly presented in these pages.

BOB BEAVER
Pastor, Christian Church of San Angelo, San Angelo, Texas

I have had the privilege of knowing Dan and Linda Wilson for a number of years. Dan is a scientist and eye surgeon who looks for accuracy and knowledge founded on solid, tangible research. It is impressive that, at the same time, he recognizes the need for the miraculous work of God intervening in our lives and relationships. He and Linda pursue the heart of God with an intense focus, which is evident in *Supernatural Marriage*. I recommend this book to all who are married and all who intend to be married. I believe this material, if applied, can revolutionize marriages all across the world.

D. LELAND PARIS
President of Youth with a Mission, Tyler, Texas
Founder/CEO of Humanitarian Relief Organizations

Wow! When the Chinese first met Dan and Linda they were very surprised because, although grandparents, they appeared as a newlywed couple. They were one in spirit, heart and mind as they daily walked as faithful Christians. I recommend this book for those who want to have the fullness of marriage that comes from being focused on the Lord. Anybody who wants to read this book will never, never be divorced.

"MISS CHOY"
Chinese leader of over 700 regional house church networks

When Dan and Linda came to Kenya in May, 2008, while in Mombasa, they taught wonderful lessons on marriage. These teachings removed walls satan had erected against our marriages. Satanic limits came off. It was like the children of Israel during the time of Gideon (Judges 7:16-21). These teachings taught by Dan and Linda will cause the glory of God to be seen in our marriages just like when the jars were broken and the torches shined brightly.

BRYSON AND NELLY NYONGESA
Church leaders, Kenya

Dedication

I dedicate this book to Linda, my lifetime partner in supernatural marriage and eternally loved friend.

Acknowledgements

Were it not for God's love, mercy, patience, and goodness, I would not have a single word to share that would encourage others in their marriages. Before my wedding with Linda I had no concept of how astounding marriage could be. God gave me far more than I asked for or imagined. Thank You, Lord, for sharing the mysteries of supernatural marriage with me, your loved child.

I am grateful to Patricia King, Bill Johnson, Robert Stearns, Keith Miller, and Brandy Helton for the significant roles they all played in helping me learn how to intimately commune with the Holy Spirit of God. Thank you, Bob Beaver, for being my pastor and friend. What a special gift I received from God through Paul Looney, who gave me my first glimpse of abundant life in Christ. All of you have blessed me more than I can put into words. Along with them, I honor Steve Mitchell, Misty Edwards, Jason Upton, Kimberly and Alberto Rivera, and Steve Swanson for ushering me and countless others into the tangible presence of God through worship.

Thank you to both Carol Martinez and the XP Publishing team for your kindness and professionalism in coordinating the production of this book, and Ryan Adair for your wise suggestions in editing. I appreciate Clay Hejl who contributed creative concepts and Steve Fryer for the design of the cover. Steve Spencer blessed the project through his instruction in theology and linguistics.

To my wife, Linda: How can I express to you the depth of my appreciation for you, the woman God chose to be my supernatural wife? God used you to introduce me to His unfathomable love and goodness. You are my greatest encourager and closest friend. This book would not have been started or completed without your inspiration, creative thoughts, wise counsel, and tireless editing. Thank you.

Contents

Foreword

by PAUL LOONEY, M.D.

Marriage is a gift. Some gifts, such as an iPod, can be unwrapped and enjoyed with very little effort. But marriage is more like receiving the gift of a piano. A piano is a beautiful, complex gift that requires commitment and hard work to master – just like marriage does. Many books on marriage are replete with concepts and exercises to provide technical skills to play well as a couple, and all of us benefit by practice and training. *Supernatural Marriage*, though, reminds us that disciplined effort and skill alone will never bring about the optimal marriage experience. A glorious marriage, like great music, requires whole-hearted engagement. It requires spirit.

Supernatural Marriage reveals that the most excellent marriages are the result of full surrender of spirit, soul, and body to the One who made the gift and who is Himself engaged with us in the playing of it. In the union of God's design, husband and wife transcend personal limitations and find inestimable worth, beauty, and grace through oneness. While some technical skill and practice are essential, the music of marriage is at its finest when infused with passion and purity that flows from the heart of God. *Supernatural Marriage* invites you into the realm of the Spirit, where all things are possible.

Dan Wilson knows what he is talking about. We have been friends for over thirty years, since medical school. More than anyone I know, Dan is rigorously honest and I count on him to tell me the truth, even when it hurts. I know no man who demonstrates love and affirmation the way he does. Even more important and admirable, though, is the way he relates to his marriage partner, Linda. While I encounter all types of couples in my work as psychiatrist and pastor, there is no one I know whose marriage mirrors the love relationship between Christ and the church more than Dan's relationship with Linda.

It has been thrilling and inspirational to watch the transformation in these two and the way it has enhanced their marriage over the years of our friendship. My wife, Teri, and I have been with these friends in all types of settings, and I am always drawn to the way of love and life that they embody. They have found something precious, and in *Supernatural Marriage* they share it.

An ophthalmologist by training, Dr. Wilson clarifies a vision beyond tolerability, functionality or even exemplary marriage. He invites us to imagine and embrace a supernatural marriage that enjoys the fullness of God's revelation and provision. Sharing deeply from his own history, Dan illuminates a path that every couple can follow to find greater harmony, energy, and grace. True oneness comes, he assures us, when partners pursue God first, rather than simply pursuing one another.

The musical score of marriage is a collaboration of woman, man and Almighty God. While there is considerable work involved, God invites every couple to play. Like a pianist, the hard work involved in making music is overshadowed by the joy of playing. While some passages must be played with relentless attention to the composer's intent, there are plenty of opportunities in a vibrant marriage for improvisation and spontaneity. Dan and Linda know how to play.

This book includes some helpful theological explanation. Theology, like music theory, is useful because it informs how we play, even though we can always enjoy the symphony without understanding all its ins and outs. Intimacy is the great reward of marriage, and God is willing to provide it even when we do not have complete understanding. Dan and Linda have given themselves to God as instruments to be played, and the book you hold affirms without question, "You can trust Him. Let Him have His way with you. Let Him play upon your soul and awaken you to His great plan for you and your marriage."

Keeping with our piano metaphor, supernatural marriage is like a wonderful duet, both partners allowing the Spirit to play through them. While in the case of an actual piano, practice prepares the musician for performance, we practice marriage more like one practices medicine. The practice is the thing itself, ever expanded and enhanced by each interaction and nuanced exchange. While a couple at the piano may practice a piece, the couple surrendered to the Lordship of Christ delights in practicing the peace. His presence is everything.

As it turns out, Dan Wilson is a marvelous musician. As a young man, I was often the beneficiary of his substantial ability. When he sat down at the baby grand, the house we shared with other medical students swelled with beautiful sounds. I enjoyed and admired his skill and passion. It lifted my spirits.

While I loved hearing him play a sonata, I find myself even more blessed by his rendition of marriage. He is truly masterful in the way he approaches his "baby" grand, in the way he expresses gratitude and appreciation for all Linda brings to the sweet and stirring music that arises from their union. Dan and Linda are crystal clear: in marriage, as in everything, we play for God. They have discovered the thrill of giving all to Him and being drawn into a stellar symphony – and all can join!

Marriage is a gift, released when two bring all they have to the One. Each partner's peculiar rhythms and cadences, chords and key signatures are gladly sacrificed to the harmonious and thrilling composition that God has written for the couple. To revel in the blessings of a supernatural marriage, we must die to what is natural, and death always occasions grief. But the resulting life is nothing short of miraculous. Remember this: there is not another couple that can play the score God has written for you and your mate. Your partnership is unique, and *Supernatural Marriage* can help you engage God and your marriage in a fresh way.

While it is true that the practice of marriage is the real deal and not merely a preparation, Dan reminds us that supernatural marriage is also a sort of dress rehearsal. Every marital union foreshadows the great day when we sit down to play with One who loves our souls passionately and without regret. And oh, what a day that will be! Imagine the music reverberating through the vault of heaven! Absolute safety, absolute surrender. Ah, the notes that will flow!

Dr. Paul Looney has been practicing as a psychiatrist for over twenty-five years. He is the director of Hidden Manna Ministries, hiddenmanna.org, through which he and his wife, Teri, provide retreats and resources for marriage and spiritual growth. He serves as teaching pastor at Fellowship of the Woodlands (Texas), where he oversees counseling and recovery ministries.

Introduction

In the spring of last year Linda and I had the privilege of leading a marriage conference for couples planning to be house parents in Mattaw Village, a new orphanage in Kitale, Kenya. The Spirit of God was noticeably present throughout the three days we spent together. As we began to teach what we had planned, God changed the conference to become what He desired it to be. What a joy! It was as if all of us were at the feet of Jesus, receiving instruction on marriage through "the Spirit of wisdom and understanding" (Isaiah 11:2).

At the close of our time together, Bryson Nyongesa, a prophet from Kenya, said to me, "You are to write a book about marriage." While at an airport on the way home from Africa, Linda and I both received a series of revelations regarding the content of the book, as well as the title – *Supernatural Marriage*. Unquestionably, we had been given a small taste of God's wisdom, along with the understanding of how to apply it. Both Linda and I were astounded as God revealed to us that day what we were to do!

Initially, the idea of writing a book seemed preposterous to us. As a full time eye surgeon, I rarely have time to read books and had never desired to write one. Yet, when God asked me to write a book communicating the goal of supernatural marriage in His Kingdom, the only appropriate response was an enthusiastic "Yes!" What seemed at first to be a daunting task has turned out to be sheer delight.

So what, exactly, is supernatural marriage? Even though it takes this entire book to answer that question well, allow me to give you a glimpse:

Supernatural marriage is the intended destiny of every marriage established within the Kingdom of God – a lofty goal consistent with the glory of heaven! No marital relationship is perfect, yet, too often we settle for seeking and barely reaching mediocre goals in marriage. This book sets the standard for marriage extremely high – not to discourage anyone but to stimulate every spouse to pursue and experience the wonders only available to marital partners who function within the supernatural realm.

Supernatural marriage is filled with the presence, passion and power of God. The glory of the Lord is constantly present and readily available to those who seek Him. When His glory invades the union of a man and woman in marriage, the result is miraculous transformation of each of them individually and of their one flesh marital relationship. Spouses involved in this kind of marital relationship are filled with peace beyond human understanding. These marital partners are enabled to be effective in ministry because they possess the fruit of the Spirit and carry favor that comes directly from the hand of God. They are abundantly blessed!

The keys to entering supernatural marriage are intimacy with God and the acceptance of His lordship. Intimately encountering the glorious presence of God changes each of us to become more and more who we were created to be. Yet, God will not allow us to regularly experience Him in this way unless true lordship has been established in us. Using these keys, every spouse has access to enter and progress, glory to glory, through the astonishing blessings God desires His children to enjoy in marriage.

Linda and I truly love being married. What a wonderful journey marriage has been for the both of us! In *Supernatural Marriage*, I will share with you concepts, truths, and philosophies of marriage we have found to be valuable throughout our twenty-eight years together. As I share our journey with you, I will also reveal very personal experiences and intimate details of our supernatural encounters with God. Intimate knowledge of God can only be received through participation in the supernatural realm. Through knowing Him we are given divine power, which provides "everything we need for life and godliness" (2 Peter 1:3). It is only as we live in His presence that we discover the wellspring of abundant life which is available to us all. Sadly, many times this divine power goes untapped by the very ones who are called to receive it and whose inheritance it is.

To know God is to love Him, because "God is love" (1 John 4:8). Linda and I have discovered that the more we are able to receive God's love, the better we are able to love each other. His supernatural love has transformed us both and has blessed us with a marriage that has far exceeded our greatest expectations. This blessing was not given because of anything we had done, but because of His own purpose and grace (2 Timothy 1:9). God has done immeasurably more than we asked for or have even imagined (Ephesians 3:20).

God's goal for your marriage is the same as His goal for ours, though our journeys may be quite different. His desire is to lovingly and purposefully bring you and your spouse into His supernatural realm, where the two of you become fully one – body, soul, and spirit – with each other and also with Him. May God bless you on this adventure of walking in the realm of the supernatural and letting your marriage be transformed by His love and power.

Part One:

FOUNDATIONS
FOR
SUPERNATURAL MARRIAGE

Chapter One

HOLY IS FUN!

"Holy is fun!" These are the words my wife, Linda, heard recently while swimming laps at our local YMCA. There was only one day left before we were to speak about marriage at The Garden Supernatural Training Center. The pressure was on. We knew something was lacking in our planned presentation, but just couldn't figure out exactly what it was. Though much effort had been made in preparation, it was clear in our spirits that something was missing. We needed fresh revelation from God and needed it quickly! We both trusted God would provide exactly what He wanted the people to hear, and were not disappointed with what He gave us that day. His amazing faithfulness would soon be shown to us again as it had been so many times throughout our lives.

Linda and I swim regularly to exercise our bodies and loosen our gradually stiffening joints. For simplicity's sake, we swim our laps while wearing masks and snorkels. Wearing these bulky devices enables us to swim as slowly or as quickly as desired without a thought as to where, when, or how to breathe. Time passed slowly during our first few swims together, unable to talk with our heads buried in the water. We all know that time goes much faster while working out when engaged in conversation with someone else. Besides that, there was really not much of interest to see on the plaster bottom of the pool!

Through the years, however, Linda and I have learned that hours of gliding through the cool water of the pool can be an enjoyable and productive time for bathing in the loving presence of the Father. While swimming laps, there are virtually no distractions from our communion with God. We can pray blessings on missionary friends living on any continent in the world or intercede for any other issue dear to our hearts. While pushing across the surface of the water, we find it very natural to commune with Jesus, our Savior and our Friend. There is no better place than the deep end of a swimming pool to ask for and receive the living water of the Holy Spirit described by Jeremiah, Zechariah, John, and in the book of Revelation. What more reasonable place to listen to the gentle whisper of God (1 Kings 19:11-12; Psalm 46:10) than in this environment of near silence?

That particular day in the pool, Linda changed her typical pattern of communion with God. Instead of actively thinking prayerful thoughts, she asked only one question of God: "What do You want to say to me for tomorrow night?" As she swam, Linda patiently waited, listening for God's response to her request. After three laps, she distinctly heard the words come into her mind and her spirit: "Holy is fun!" A bit confused, her immediate response was the silent question of what that phrase meant. Again she heard clearly in her mind and spirit the same phrase: "Holy is fun!"

GOD'S PLAYGROUND

The Holy Spirit brought to her mind a sermon she had heard years before. The speaker related a story about a school playground adjacent to a busy city street. There was no fence separating the two, and both children and teachers could sense the danger that was present. In this atmosphere, kindergarten students remained very close to their teacher during recess instead of playing in the big open field. Although this assured their safety, it also deprived them of the many areas and activities available on the playground. The school children were unable to fully enjoy recess because the playground felt treacherous and dangerous to them.

The school leaders, aware of the risk of having children play so close to the street, had a sturdy fence constructed around the borders of the playground. Soon the small children, who were previously reluctant to leave their teacher, were running, bouncing balls, swinging, and exuberantly playing on every square inch of the property. They were full of joy and laughter because they had a truly safe place to play where there was no danger from the cars being so close. What had seemed scary to them was now fun because of the barrier that separated them from the dangerous traffic on the street.

Marriage is very much like that properly fenced playground. In the written word of the Bible, by direct revelation and through the personal leading of the Holy Spirit, God establishes wise, strong, incredibly important barriers around His children's marital playground. All activity within these secured boundaries is righteous and good, conforming to God's perfect will. Anything outside of these boundaries is unholy, unrighteous, and outside of His will. Everything outside of these boundaries is the street we're not allowed to play in because of the risk of danger involved.

HOLINESS OF GOD AND MARRIAGE

God is always completely holy, and it is His will that the marriage covenant be completely holy as well. Holiness is the essence of who He is and what He is. He cannot be anything less than holy because that is who He is. Because it is impossible for Him to change (Malachi 3:6), He cannot and will not act outside of His character. And because we are created in His image, His desire is for us to become like Him, as completely as possible, both as individuals and as marriage partners.

As we grow in holiness, we honor God as our Creator and honor the beauty and perfection of His plan. Our holiness greatly pleases the Father. In fact, He demands that we become holy, just as He is holy. This is why in establishing the Law with the children of Israel, God repeatedly told Moses, "Speak to the entire assembly of Israel and say to them: 'Be holy because I, the Lord your God, am holy'" (Leviticus 19:2, 11:44-45).

Similar to the fenced school playground, the covenant of marriage is a place of complete safety. Because God is holy and He demands nothing but holiness from us as individuals, then we can only conclude that He longs for holiness in our marriages as well. The writer of Hebrews states it like this: "Marriage should be honored by all, and the marriage bed kept pure, for God will judge the adulterer and all the sexually immoral" (Hebrews 13:4).

It has rightly been said, "There is no place safer than the center of God's will." The protective boundaries of marriage were established long ago by God and demonstrated in the original marriage in the Garden of Eden (Genesis 2). The foundations of God's fences were laid with His unchanging love for us, and the structure of these barriers was erected using wisdom and understanding. They are built of eternally unchanging truth and demonstrate, both to the world and to us, the absolute goodness of God. They were not laid because God didn't want us to have fun; but the boundaries were erected so we could have the most fun possible in the context of marriage. We have to remember that holy is fun!

A marriage truly connected to the holiness of God is an amazing thing. In this kind of relationship we can let down all our defenses and just *be* instead of always *doing* and trying to perform. We fulfill the destiny God created us to enjoy as we walk in the holiness of marriage. In this place all is freely shared and no barrier exists between husband and wife. There is no fear about what the other person might think, nor is there any doubt concerning the motivations of each other's actions. In God's playground called marriage, we are encouraged to love deeply and freely, to laugh and to play, without fear of the dangers that lie outside of these God-ordained boundaries.

There has been no restraint in the Father's demonstration of love to us through the giving of Jesus. It was only because of His great love for us and His desire to be in relationship with us, that the Father gave Jesus to break the power of sin and to put us back in right relationship with Him. "For God so loved the world that he gave his one and only Son, that whoever believes in him shall not perish but have eternal life" (John 3:16). Paul asks, "He who did not spare his own Son, but gave him up for us all – how will he not also, along with him, graciously give us all things?" (Romans 8:32).

Likewise, He urges us in marriage to have no restraint as we verbalize and act out our love for each other. When we walk in the boundaries God has given us for marriage, there is nothing that is held back in the mutual giving of love between husband and wife.

FRUIT THROUGH INTIMACY WITH JESUS

The playground of marriage is designed to be consistently filled with the fruit of the Spirit. Paul gives us a list of what this fruit of the Spirit consists of when he writes: "But the fruit of the Spirit is love, joy, peace, patience, kindness, goodness, faithfulness, gentleness and self-control. Against such things there is no law" (Galatians 5:22-23). The description of this fruit is simply a list of God's more prominent attributes. These characteristics are fruit produced in our lives by the Spirit of God. Because we are commanded to be holy as God is holy, this fruit is only the outflow of God's character being produced in us and outworking through us. This list of fruit illustrates how God treats others in intimate relationships and it also establishes the gold standard of how we should deal with each other in our relationships – especially marriage.

God's qualities and fruit are planted and cultivated in us by the Holy Spirit when we allow Him to take up residence in our hearts. The characteristics of this fruit are not ways of living that we learn about and strive for, but supernaturally revealed attributes that are transferred to our inner man. Spiritual fruit will never be produced through human effort alone. It cannot be successfully manufactured or copied. It can be acquired only when it is given by the Father and received by His children as a gift.

The sad fact is that the fruit of the Spirit is often absent from marriages because the individuals involved have been unsuccessful at intimately connecting with the Holy Spirit, who is the only possible source of the fruit. It seems this would be intuitively obvious, but to many it is not. In fact, Galatians 5:22 is generally taught in churches using a cognitive approach, which is essentially a humanistic presentation of how to receive this gift through human understanding and effort. We are told that if we try to live in peace, smile regularly, be good when others are watching, and exhibit self-control (except when temptation occasionally becomes too strong), these qualities will be easier for us to walk in ... most of the time. This kind of teaching is powerless, theologically incorrect, and exceedingly dangerous. It is in direct opposition to what Paul is saying in this passage. The fruit produced by the Spirit is manifest in us because it changes who we are as individuals – the very core of our being.

The truth is that the fruit of the Spirit is a portion of the "streams of living water" (John 7:38) that will flow from within us and from within our marriages when we have received and are walking in the holiness of God. However, these streams will flow only when we are intimately connected to Jesus, the Father, and the Holy Spirit (2 Corinthians 13:14). When we passionately pursue the Holy Spirit's presence in our lives and in our marriages, we honor Jesus' prayer: "May they also be in us so that the world may believe that you have sent me" (John 17:21). It is His plan that the world will believe in Jesus because we, His disciples, are so intimately connected to the Father that we produce the character qualities of the Father in our everyday lives. These character qualities of the Father are also known as the fruit of the Spirit.

This fruit cannot be be mimicked for any real length of time. It is possible to fake the outward manifestation of the fruit of the Spirit for some time, but sooner or later, who we really are will come out. It is impossible to experience any form of living water in our marriages simply by trying harder or solely through more study of the Bible. The fruit of the Spirit can only be received as a spiritual gift, which is a divine impartation. It shows up in our lives as evidence of its supernatural implantation into the very core of our being. It literally transforms who we are in our very heart and soul.

Once we have supernaturally received this gift, we actually possess the fruit of the Spirit. It is ours and becomes a very significant part of who we are. This is consistent with the will of God, because the fruit of the Spirit is His character qualities. It is, in a very real sense, who He is. The Father wants us to mature and grow up to become like Him. This is why Jesus told us to be "perfect, therefore, as your heavenly Father is perfect" (Matthew 5:48), and why Paul told the Ephesians to be "imitators of God ... as dearly loved children" (Ephesians 5:1). They didn't tell us to expect something we could never attain to – but because they told us to pursue being like the Father, then it has to be assumed it is possible to imitate our Father in heaven. Every good father has the desire for his children to grow up and be a good representation of him, and God is certainly no exception.

SAFETY IN THE MARRIAGE PLAYGROUND

When the fruit of the Spirit is clearly possessed by both spouses in a supernatural marriage, the Father is doubly honored and doubly pleased. This is because He is honored and pleased with both husband and wife. With these qualities consistently demonstrated in their lives, the living water flows freely in their relationship. The playground is completely safe when God's perfectly planned boundaries are solidly in place. Their love for each other is without measure, their joy together is unrestrained, they walk in peace that passes understanding, and they are patient and kind to each other, even when imperfections creep in. It is always assumed the other's intentions are good, though to the human mind it may seem otherwise. There is absolute faithfulness with no thought, hint, or joke of infidelity. Harshness has no place in the covenant of marriage, and gentleness prevails in their dealings with one another because self-control is consistently present.

What a wonderful, safe place to live and play! Living in supernatural marriage beautifully displays what Jesus asked the Father for when He prayed, "Your kingdom come, your will be done on earth as it is in heaven" (Matthew 6:10). Does this sound idealistic, far-fetched, or even extreme? Does the concept of supernatural marriage sound impossible for you in your particular situation? Even people with good intentions may tell you that no married couple should hope to enjoy the glory of heaven while still living on earth. Jesus, however, looks at you and says, "With man this is impossible, but with God *all* things are possible" (Matthew 19:26, emphasis mine). Do you believe that Jesus only said this, or do you believe Jesus really meant it? And do you believe He meant it for *you* and for *your* marriage?

Linda and I are confident this kind of marriage is possible. It is not possible through your own striving and trying to be a better spouse. No, supernatural marriage will only come as you get focused on the right thing – living in communion with God on a daily basis. It is only as we stay connected to the Father through intimacy that we can demonstrate the fruit of God's Spirit in our marital relationships.

Linda and I have experienced unexpected and amazing joy in our marriage. The Holy Spirit has brought us into realms of intimacy with God and with each other we didn't know existed before. Allowing the supernatural work of God to enter and transform our natural lives has been the key to unlocking marital life far beyond what we asked for or even imagined. It has occurred according to His power and might, not from striving on our own. "Now to him who is able to do immeasurably more than all we ask or imagine, according to his power that is at work within us" (Ephesians 3:20).

Transformation of marriage toward the safe playground it was intended to be is available to any believer who allows it to become the true desire of their heart. Psalm 20:4 says, "May [God] give you the desire of your heart and make all your plans succeed." The psalmist also declares, "Delight yourself in the Lord; and he will give you the desires of your heart" (37:4). We can be better prepared for holy matrimony through Bible studies, counseling, and a mental understanding of what this concept means. But anything that is holy can only be perceived and received in the supernatural realm – as a work of God's Spirit and His grace. Linda was right – there is no doubt about it – holy is fun!

Chapter Two

THE TENSION OF TWO REALMS

*I*n this chapter I would like to discuss how I'm using the words "supernatural" and "natural," and the tension that exists between the two realms. There is so much controversy with these words in the church today – the term "supernatural" sometimes carries negative connotations with it, so it will be helpful to define how I use them. That way there will be no misunderstanding throughout the rest of this book.

I do believe that there is a natural realm in which we live, and there is a supernatural realm that exists outside of the natural realm. Jesus alluded to both of them in His prayer to the Father: "My prayer is not that you take them out of the world but that you protect them from the evil one" (John 17:15). We are to pray for the realm of heaven to invade the realm of earth: "Our Father in heaven, hallowed be your name, your kingdom come, your will be done on earth as it is in heaven" (Matthew 6:9-10). We are also to live as citizens of another world while maintaining our life in this present world: "But our citizenship is in heaven. And we eagerly await a Savior from there, the Lord Jesus Christ" (Philippians 3:20).

TWO REALMS COMPETING

Nature can be defined as the external, observable, measurable universe that surrounds us. It is thought to exist within the constraints of time. According to *Merriam-Webster's Dictionary*, the natural realm consists of those things that occur "in conformity with the ordinary course of nature: not marvelous or supernatural." We are continually and keenly aware of the natural realm that surrounds us, making it easy to discuss and understand. In fact, science would lead us to believe that reality does not extend beyond the limitations of the natural physical world, which are the things that are perceivable with our senses and explainable by human reason.

Secular thinking within Western culture, and even in the Western church, is strongly rooted in this quest for scientific, tangible truth. As a whole, our society does not accept the validity or importance of human experiences outside the natural realm which cannot be explained by human reason. The intense suspicion of our society towards supernatural experiences is quite evident from our language choices. "Supernatural" carries the connotation of a strong bias against the reasonableness of our participation in this realm. In *Merriam-Webster's Thesaurus*, words offered as synonymous with *supernatural* include "weird," "bizarre," and even "unnatural."

Because of this, many Christian churches and institutions teach and discuss the supernatural events in the Bible from a purely historical perspective without any thought or expectancy of God currently acting in supernatural ways. Most acknowledge that in the past God performed great signs and wonders through mortal men.

Many also believe that even greater demonstrations of the supernatural are coming when Jesus returns. However, it is often taught that in *the present time,* our lives are almost completely restricted to the natural, physical realm.

The outcome is that many believers tend to believe the falsehood that although we are supernaturally saved by the grace of God, all of the other experiences with God in this realm are dangerous and should be completely avoided. How tragic this is! If the God of the Bible did supernatural events throughout history and will do them in the future, then why do we believe the lie that He is not moving in our present time?

God did not do miracles for thousands of years, then suddenly stop doing them in our time. Far from it, He is a God of the supernatural, who longs to communicate with us just as He did with the people we read about in the Scriptures. Supernatural experiences with God are not something that should be feared, talked down, or altogether avoided; rather, they should be embraced by all Christians everywhere as present reality!

CONNECTING WITH GOD'S SPIRIT

God began the creation of the world using His supernatural power; He created the first man, Adam, in His image and likeness. The Trinity, in discussing the creation of man, said, "Let us make man in our image, in our likeness and let them rule..." Then the account states: "So God created man in his own image, in the image of God he created him; male and female he created them" (Genesis 1:26-27). All human beings were made to be like God in many ways. God is Spirit (John 4:24) and so are we; thus, there is no question that participation in the supernatural realm can and should be normal to us as children of God.

Because God created us in His image, we have a spirit as well. When we commune with God, it is our spirit touching His Spirit. "God is spirit, and his worshipers must worship in spirit and in truth" (John 4:24). When we connect with God, we are connecting with Him via our spirits – not with some other aspect of our being.

For Linda and me, experiencing the Holy Spirit in the center of our marriage has been the key to unlocking the door to more fully enjoying our life together. The supernatural touch of God has brought us the joy of experiencing sweet intimacy with Him and also with each other. We have learned that His ways, which are supernatural, are not our ways, which are natural (Isaiah 55:8). The more we grow and walk with Him, the more we also are being taught that we live by faith in the supernatural realm, not by sight, which resides in the realm of the natural (2 Corinthians 5:7).

It is completely normal for us, as ambassadors of the Kingdom of God, to regularly participate in this supernatural realm, and it should be every believer's experience. As with most things inherited from Satan, who is the "father of lies" (John 8:44), the common perception of the supernatural being weird, bizarre, or unnatural is actually the opposite of the truth. There is nothing more normal than a loved child of God intimately connecting spirit to Spirit with Abba Father. The more bizarre thing is trying to relate to God on a rational level only.

In holy matrimony, we also relate spirit to spirit with our spouses. Since God created us and placed us in a covenant of marriage, it is completely predictable that as we become more intimately connected with God, we are also enabled to more intimately relate to each other. This applies to both our physical, natural relationship, and our spiritual, supernatural relationship within marriage. Both husband and wife can become more completely "one flesh" (Genesis 2:24) through the presence of the Holy Spirit dwelling within them. There is a bond that takes place in the ceremony of marriage that is purely supernatural, and only God can accomplish it. There is a union of spirits between husband and wife where the two individuals literally become "one flesh." When Adam first saw the woman who had been taken from his rib, he said, "This is now bone of my bones and flesh of my flesh" (Genesis 2:23). Then it is said, "For this reason a man will leave his father and mother and be united to his wife, and they will become one flesh" (Genesis 2:24).

SCIENTIFIC "FACTS" AS OPPOSED TO
SUPERNATURAL REALITY

It is amazing to me how firmly we hold to many scientific assumptions in light of innumerable facts that later turn out to be far from true. For example, the theory of evolution is now regularly taught and even legislated as a proven fact, which, of course, it is not if we hold the biblical record to be true. In the past, man believed for years that the earth was flat, only to have this firm conviction shattered in the face of new, experienced knowledge.

Another interesting example is found in the description of the optic nerve in the back of the eye. Because of the limitations of the instruments used to examine the eye during the 1800s, doctors believed and taught that the center of the optic nerve head was a convex protrusion. As medical instruments improved through the years, that well-known fact was reversed to reflect the discovery that the center of the optic nerve (now called the optic cup) is actually concave.

Scientific "facts" often change with time. But spiritual, supernatural realities are unchanging. Because supernatural realities come from God, we know they are like Jesus, who "is the same yesterday and today and forever" (Hebrews 13:8) – they never change. Truth always supersedes fact.

The supernatural realm includes many things that are not measurable, controllable, or easily grasped by the human mind. Furthermore, although our world is extremely time oriented, time has little meaning in the supernatural realm because it exists in an eternal, spiritual domain.

God continually lives in the supernatural realm, as do the powers of darkness that attempt to oppose Him. Our experiences in the supernatural realm can occur as a result of our participation with either Satan's kingdom of darkness or God's glorious Kingdom of light. I am using the word "supernatural" throughout this book to reference spiritual interactions with the true and living God. Although there are many spiritual experiences that are out there, many from God and many of them demonic, I am primarily talking about experiencing God in the supernatural realm. These experiences can dramatically change our marriages.

OVERLAPPING REALMS

In our minds we tend to compartmentalize the concepts of the natural and supernatural, making them mutually exclusive. Growing up in the world and being trained as a scientist, I once viewed these two realms in this way. I had a tendency to exclude from my belief system supernatural events that conflicted with what I could observe in the physical, natural realm. But the more experiences I have in the supernatural realm, the more overlap I recognize between the two realms. Encountering the glory of the Lord causes fundamental change in our understanding of both the natural and supernatural realms.

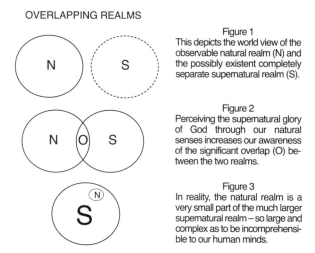

OVERLAPPING REALMS

Figure 1
This depicts the world view of the observable natural realm (N) and the possibly existent completely separate supernatural realm (S).

Figure 2
Perceiving the supernatural glory of God through our natural senses increases our awareness of the significant overlap (O) between the two realms.

Figure 3
In reality, the natural realm is a very small part of the much larger supernatural realm – so large and complex as to be incomprehensible to our human minds.

Human Talent

The overlap between the natural and supernatural can be found in what we express as human talent. Talent is used when we describe increased capacity, aptitude, or gifting in a particular area of natural human functioning; it is the ability to do something particularly well. Talents are given to us through the will of our Sovereign Creator, who made each of us exactly the way He desired. We are fully equipped to accomplish our assigned task in His eternal Kingdom. Talents are thoughtfully and carefully given to us for noble purposes and can be powerful tools for the achievement of our destiny.

God will allow us to use these talents in the natural world even without submission to His lordship. We often see extremely talented individuals flaunting their hedonistic lifestyles while they scoff at the One who gave them the abilities that made them famous; yet He does not withdraw these divinely given gifts. What may not be obvious, however, is that when these gifts are used without honoring the One who gave them, they will never be developed into their full potential. They remain relatively immature, even though they can be impressive talents to those who observe them. Talent of any kind is dramatically enhanced when the person possessing it receives anointing from God and the talent becomes sanctified, or set apart, for God's use.

Sanctified Human Talent

In the context of a believer who understands his talent is a gift from God, it is another story altogether. God releases a portion of His glory into the individual believer. That person's talent is shifted from the natural realm into the supernatural realm. Talent perceivable in the natural realm is released to its destiny by the enhancing effect of the supernatural. The glory of the Lord shines out through that individual believer as he accomplishes things that would not be humanly possible. Functioning in the supernatural realm becomes natural to believers through the presence and anointing of God. The supernatural touch of God on your life doesn't mean you act strangely, as if you are not part of this earth. The fact is that we are in this world for a particular purpose and time in history. We were put here to do what only we can do.

The effect of supernatural anointing is similar to that of a catalyst in chemistry. A catalyst is an element or molecule that speeds up the rate of a chemical reaction, increasing it by tenfold or a thousandfold. Without a catalyst, some molecular reactions proceed so slowly that nothing useful is accomplished. But when a catalyst is added, the same molecules react efficiently and effectively, producing in abundance exactly what the chemist desires.

When God chooses to release His supernatural anointing, sharing His glory with the body, soul, and spirit of a man or woman, that person's talents are "catalyzed." Natural abilities are amplified and enhanced. He or she is able to function more easily and more effectively than what was previously possible – what had been impossible now becomes possible. The natural man or woman truly becomes supernatural when touched by the anointing and power of God. When we allow this divine process to take place in us, we accomplish things far beyond our natural human abilities. Others can also see the glory of the Lord shining out from us and we reflect glory back to God, who is the ultimate source of all good things.

Sanctified Gifts In North Korea

Linda and I have a friend who has worked for years providing humanitarian relief in the Democratic Peoples' Republic of Korea, which is also known as North Korea. We have worked with him from time to time to provide medical care to some of the poorest people on earth. When working in North Korea, we are not allowed to speak or teach about God to the citizens there because of the strict laws against it. In the natural realm, we cooperate with the North Koreans' rules. But they have no way to control us in the realm of the supernatural.

Nothing can stop the glory of the Lord from shining out of our eyes, our smiles, and our hearts. When I am there, I even lay hands on my patients' heads and pray for them, both in English and in tongues. As I examine these patients, I impart to them peace that passes understanding and a deep desire for the truth and goodness of God. These people are cruelly oppressed, yet still able to perceive and receive spiritual realities in the supernatural realm.

One patient we worked with in North Korea had a son who was engaged to be married. He had sensed the glory of God in our Christian friend[1] and he knew our friend had enjoyed a beautiful and loving relationship with his wife for many years. Like most fathers, this North Korean man wanted to bless his son, so he asked

---

[1] Name omitted for safety reasons.

our friend to advise his son as to how he too might enjoy a long and joyful marriage.

Our friend was restricted from speaking of God in that tightly controlled communist country, but he agreed to provide premarital counseling. Without specifically mentioning God or the Bible, he taught biblical concepts of how a man and woman should relate to each other in marriage. The teaching amazed the young man, as he had never heard anything like it before. As they finished their last session together, our friend was asked, "Where did you learn these things filled with such profound wisdom?"

The Holy Spirit supernaturally inspired the words written in the Bible; therefore they are filled with the Spirit of wisdom and the Spirit of understanding. They were very useful and inspiring to the North Korean man, as something inside him told him they were not words inspired from the earth. He realized a supernatural element to them, whether he could describe it or not. What a blessing for him and his marriage that he received them! Even richer blessings are available to spouses whose knowledge of God's Word is enhanced by the presence of the Spirit of God within them.

A THREE-STRANDED CORD IS NOT QUICKLY BROKEN

The writer of Ecclesiastes wrote, "Though one may be overpowered, two can defend themselves. A cord of three strands is not quickly broken" (4:12). A very helpful aid in my understanding of this verse is a visual demonstration of this passage used by Dr. Paul Looney, a Christian psychiatrist who leads Hidden Manna Ministries. For years in their One Flesh marriage seminars, Paul and his wife, Teri, have provided each spouse with a brightly colored strand. The color given is specific to each person's personality type and way of relating with others. The two spouses weave together their two colored strands, combining them with a third golden strand representing the supernatural presence of God in their marriage. Together, the three strands form a cord that is both strong and beautiful.

I used to think of this third strand as the truths and ways of God as taught in the Bible that could be lived out in marriage. Of course, I was aware of the reality of the Holy Spirit and the supernatural realm, but I found it difficult to connect with Him on this level in practical ways. As a result, I related to Linda based on my mental understanding of biblical concepts. Even though this was very useful and good, just as it was for the young man receiving premarital counseling in North Korea, it was not God's highest goal for our marriage. If husband and wife interact with each other only in ways based on human understanding, even if it is understanding founded upon principles revealed in the Scriptures, their marital relationship will be limited to the natural realm and thus exclude the glorious revelations and experiences available in the supernatural realm.

The presence of God's Holy Spirit is the key to transformation, both in our personal lives and in our marriages. Supernaturally experiencing God changes our vision of the future, our purpose in life, the way we think, and the way we act with God and with our spouses. It enhances our ability to love and receive love. As we carry within us the glory of God, we are empowered to live beyond natural constraints. When we learn to live consistently in the supernatural realm, nothing remains the same. Our perception of the temporal changes and our understanding of eternal things are greatly enhanced.

Within supernatural marriage, both spouses recognize they are eternal beings living in temporary surroundings. Just three years ago, things in the natural realm seemed so real and significant to both Linda and me. But in surprising and beautiful ways, God began showing us that temporal things must no longer dictate our purpose or our plan in life. We began to live much differently, realizing that "our citizenship is in heaven. And we eagerly await a Savior from there, the Lord Jesus Christ" (Philippians 3:20). Without question, the eternal will triumph over the temporal. Satan's kingdom of this world will be replaced by the supernatural Kingdom of our God, for "the kingdom of the world has become the kingdom of our Lord and of his Christ, and he will reign for ever and ever" (Revelation 11:15).

Linda and I framed our three woven strands and placed them on the wall of our bedroom. We see them daily as a reminder that only the golden strand of God's glory in our marriage can draw us as one flesh into the destiny He has placed before us. Our desire is that through God's supernatural presence His will be done in our marriage on earth, just as it is in heaven (Matthew 6:10).

PERCEIVING THE SUPERNATURAL

For most of my life, I believed in my mind that our supernatural God rarely interacted with someone in the natural realm. I was taught that although they did this often in Bible times, it would be an extremely rare occurrence, until the return of Jesus, for Him to do it again. I trusted that the Holy Spirit was real, but I had never seen much evidence of supernatural things in myself or in others. I had a mental conceptualization of spiritual things, but was much more confident in the reality of the physical world around me that I could see than the supernatural realm that I couldn't see. It was like I was living the opposite of Paul's words: "So we fix our eyes not on what is seen, but on what is unseen. For what is seen is temporary, but what is unseen is eternal" (2 Corinthians 4:18).

After I turned fifty, however, God allowed me for the first time in my life to knowingly experience His supernatural presence in my natural body.[2] Since that time I have had numerous tangible encounters with the Holy Spirit that have radically changed my understanding of what is real. I now see the supernatural realm as more authentic than the natural realm. For example, I now perceive the tangible, manifested presence of God as more real than the laptop computer with which I write these words. This laptop will one day be no more, whereas God's presence will exist throughout all of time and into eternity. There is nothing more real to me than God.

God revealed Himself to Moses as, "I am who I am." When Moses was wondering what to tell the Israelites as to who sent him, God responded by saying that this is what he should declare to them: "I AM has sent me to you" (Exodus 3:14). Our supernatural God lived long before the beginning of time. I AM exists "from everlasting to everlasting" (1 Chronicles 16:36). As a Spirit being, He was forever present prior to the creation of the natural realm (Genesis 1:1). He will continue to live forever after this physical world is gone. Therefore, He and His supernatural Kingdom are truly much more real than any of the natural, created things encountered with the five senses. The natural things we currently experience are imperfect and only temporary. Their existence is fleeting, and they will be replaced by a new creation that is perfect and eternal.

The truth that we are in Him and He is in us (John 17:21) demonstrates the complex overlapping of the supernatural and the natural realms. The glory of the Lord was shown through the perfection of creation. The separation between the natural and the

---

[2] I share this in detail in chapter 4, "Texas Ablaze: Our Journey into Supernatural Encounters with God."

supernatural did not exist in the Garden of Eden. Adam and Eve saw God in everything that surrounded them and experienced His intimate presence in their normal day-to-day lives. Genesis reveals what seems to be an everyday occurrence when it mentions the Lord coming down to walk among them in the cool of the day (Genesis 3:8).

God's goal in our marriages is that we be completely one flesh – body, soul, and spirit – with each other and with Him. The artificial separation between the natural and supernatural realms is a scheme devised by Satan after the original sin of Adam and Eve, as a way of preventing true communion and intimacy between man, woman, and God. The destiny of supernatural marriage is to reestablish in our everyday lives the complete oneness experienced by Adam, Eve, and God in the Garden of Eden.

During the six days of creation, God beautifully demonstrated "the Spirit of wisdom and of understanding, the Spirit of counsel and of power" (Isaiah 11:2). Repeatedly, He said His creation was "good" (Genesis 1:4, 10, 12, 18, 21, 25). But not until He made the man and woman in His own image does He say, "It was *very* good" (Genesis 1:31, emphasis mine). In my imagination I hear Him shouting these words with joy to the farthest galaxies in the universe as they are shaken by the sound of His voice.

Marriage was God's most glorious creation. In it He combined flesh and spirit, natural and supernatural, the perfect lover and the perfectly loved. Nothing was held back and nothing was left out. He created something that had never been before, but always would be. He put the glory of the Creator into that which was gloriously created.

SUPERNATURAL IS A MUST!

In supernatural marriage, our goal is to be so closely linked to God that we can receive, shine out, and reflect back His glory. The normal result of such intimate connectedness is that we are transformed by His presence to become holy, just as He is holy (Leviticus 11:45). Holy matrimony, then, occurs when the glorious presence of God is physically and spiritually exhibited in both spouses and a "one flesh" union is formed.

In those marriages, God hovers over both partners, just like the Holy Spirit hovered over the waters during creation (Genesis 1:2). When the two come together in His name, He is there with them (Matthew 18:20). They are in Jesus and He is in them, just as He is in the Father (John 14:20). In a marriage experiencing the glory of the risen Savior, husband and wife can as one flesh rise "up with Christ and be seated with him in the heavenly realms" (Ephesians 2:6). This is an awesome opportunity and a wonderful goal for us.

Paul wrote:

However, as it is written: "No eye has seen, no ear has heard, no mind has conceived what God has prepared for those who love him" – but God has revealed it to us by his Spirit.

The Spirit searches all things, even the deep things of God. For who among men knows the thoughts of a man except the man's spirit within him? In the same way no one knows the thoughts of God except the Spirit of God. We have not received the spirit of the world but the Spirit who is from God, that we may understand what God has freely given us. This is what we speak, not in words taught us by human wisdom but in words taught by the Spirit, expressing spiritual truths in spiritual words. The man without the Spirit does not accept the things that come from the Spirit of God, for they are foolishness to him, and he cannot understand them, because they are spiritually discerned. The spiritual man makes judgments about all things, but he himself is not subject to any man's judgment:

"For who has known the mind of the Lord that he may instruct him?" But we have the mind of Christ.

– 1 Corinthians 2:9–16

Holy matrimony cannot exist on a God-given level without participation in the supernatural realm. It is birthed through faith in God and an honest desire for the things of His Kingdom. Some growth and partial comprehension of it can be obtained through verbal description and careful instruction. However, marriage will never blossom into its intended splendor without entering the supernatural realm.

The deep things of God cannot be taught and comprehended by the natural mind; they must be received in our spirits by faith. We will never really know God in His fullness until we experience Him spirit to Spirit. As "deep calls out to deep," so our spirits call out to Him (Psalm 42:7). Without knowing God, it is impossible to enter into the marriage covenant in the way He desired and created it to be. Sure, we can get married and live in decent harmony with our spouses without God's involvement in our lives. But if our marriages are to become fully what God intends them to be, we must take delivery of "what God has prepared for those who love him," which can only be revealed by His Spirit. We must be tangibly connected to the Spirit of God, "that we may understand what God has freely given us." The things He teaches us must be spiritually discerned, for only through the supernatural realm can we have "the mind of Christ."

From the beginning, God intended marriage to be supernatural. He desires to be in the center of your marriage, making it full of love, joy, peace, patience, kindness, and goodness. There is no better way to enjoy the fruit of the Spirit than to invite the Holy Spirit into your life and your marriage, making both holy and sanctified. There is no greater joy in life than that which comes through participation in a supernatural marriage. In this kind of relationship you will experience absolute peace that can be neither explained nor understood, but is incredibly real. This is the way God created marriage to be – completely good, completely satisfying, completely filled with His love and His glory, completely supernatural, and completely holy.

Chapter Three

LONGING FOR SPRINGTIME

IS IT SPRINGTIME YET?

As a small child I became aware that God had placed within my innermost being a strong and relentless desire for Him. It was a small seed God planted in soil He knew would be fertile. As long as I can remember I have known of the existence of this seed deep in my spirit and hoped to discover the purpose it was to play out in my life. I have felt this seed sprouting deep in the soil of my soul, slowly yet steadily establishing a root structure secure in the truths of God. Since it was God who placed the seed there, only time would tell how quickly He would cause it to sprout up.

Root structures are not visible to the naked eye without digging into the ground. Even though you can't see them without further investigation, the root structures are very real, quite alive, and completely essential if growth is to burst forth in the life-giving sunshine of spring. Yet, as the years passed there was little visible evidence of growth in my spiritual life. Though I knew my life was not as full as it could be, I truly believed that abundant life with God could come at any time. It was a promise from Jesus Himself: "I have come that they may have life, and have it to the full" (John 10:10). The joyous miracle of exuberant spring growth was unquestionably coming ... but when?

Turning fifty was a time to consider my half-century of living on this earth. God had given me every physical and emotional blessing I could have ever imagined. He gave me a faithful wife who loved me with all her heart, two boys who had grown into men of God with true integrity, and twenty years of working at a vocation I honestly enjoyed. I had known about Jesus from the earliest years I could possibly remember, and my faith in God was real. I tried to honor God and trusted Him most of the time, but my love for God was more in my head than in my heart. Although I desired intimacy with the Holy Spirit and to connect with Him on a deeper level, I had absolutely no concept of how to meet or fulfill that desire. I knew how to love my wife and knew reasonably well how to love my children. Yet all these years something had blocked my ability to deeply love the One who is, in Himself, the essence of love, for John writes of Him: "God is love" (1 John 4:8).

It seemed as if I were stuck in an eternal winter. I had been successfully planted in the Lord. Unlike the seed sown in rocky places Jesus speaks of in Mark 4, my roots had grown deep through the years. However, even a plant that is rooted well in fertile soil does not produce its abundant crop while trapped under the permafrost. I was ready for abundant life with the One who initiated life, anxious to get on with the purposes for which I was created. I wanted to go beyond knowing about God and talking about Jesus, to craving to "taste and see that the Lord is good" (Psalm 34:8). I wanted to fully experience who He was, is, and always will be. I longed for the yoke of winter to be destroyed by the joyful, exhilarating growth of spring. I wanted what the writer of the Song of Solomon talked about when he wrote: "For the winter is past, the rain is over and gone. The flowers are springing up and the time of the singing of birds has come. Yes, spring is here" (2:11-12, TLB).

ENCOUNTER WITH DELIVERANCE

Then, several years ago, Linda went through an afternoon of teaching and prayer focused on deliverance. She later told me amazing things about what happened. The Holy Spirit brought to her mind events from childhood which had never really been dealt with or healed. She was enabled to forgive every hurt the Holy Spirit had brought to her mind and repent for participating in things that were not of God. She was freed from the control of fear of man and also from pride. Linda related to me how she could feel demons that had oppressed her for years leave as they prayed that afternoon. That night she felt a deep sense of inner peace and an increased level of confidence that she had never sensed before. No doubt – something of great significance had occurred within her during the events of the afternoon!

Linda had always been a gentle person who possessed the ability to love people deeply. The fruit of the Spirit was nearly always evident in her life and everyone she came into contact with could sense the love of God flowing through her. Yet, following her time of deliverance, I could sense her joy, peace, patience, and kindness had all entered a new and higher level. She had loved me deeply for years, but suddenly she loved me even more than I had ever previously sensed from her. Nothing outwardly seemed to change. But there was something deeper that I couldn't explain. We had always enjoyed our physical intimacy together since the time we had been married. But somehow, even that part of our relationship improved dramatically.

I wasn't surprised that Linda had been blessed through her experience of deliverance, as most people feel a deep sense of joy and peace for a time after a period of intense communion with God. I purposefully watched her week after week to see how long the spiritual high would last. To my amazement, even after months it did not wear off – she was permanently changed by God's power and presence! We both liked it! I pondered the delightful change that had occurred in Linda and I secretly thought to myself, "Could this help someone like me?" At first she pressured me to go through deliverance, but wisely backed off to allow the Holy Spirit to lead me into the experience. Because she had experienced such a profound change since going through her own deliverance, out of her love for me she wanted me to experience the same. But her words were not what softened my heart. It was the glory of the Lord shining brightly each day from my wife's radiant face, relentlessly drawing me into His plan for my life.

Controversy of Deliverance

Deliverance seems to be a source of some controversy in many churches today. This shouldn't be surprising because controversy even surrounded Christ as He performed deliverance on many.

The words and miracles performed by Jesus stirred up disagreement among the religious leaders of His day as well. They didn't believe a man of God had authority or power to cast out demons, so they said the act of deliverance could only be empowered by Satan himself. The Pharisees, the religious leaders of the day, claimed that it was "only by Beelzebub, the prince of demons, that this fellow drives out demons" (Matthew 12:24). But Jesus responded to them, "Every kingdom divided against itself will be ruined, and every city or household divided against itself will not stand. If Satan drives out Satan, he is divided against himself. How then can his kingdom stand? ... But if I drive out demons by the Spirit of God, then the kingdom of God has come upon you" (Matthew 12:25-28).

The pharisaical argument spoken to Jesus makes no more sense now than it did two thousand years ago. Without question, my wife, Linda, experienced profound and persistent freedom through the supernatural act of deliverance.

Six months later, I was fully convinced that this experience could help me in my life. I called Jeff and Brandy Helton, who are my special friends involved in deliverance ministry in San Angelo, Texas, and asked them to lead me through deliverance, very similar to what my wife went through. We spent several hours together while others prayed passionately for the three of us as we were meeting. The Spirit of Jesus touched me that night in a way I had never been touched before. I was delivered from much oppression and began to live with more confidence and joy. God blessed me with a remarkably improved ability to commune with Him in the spiritual realm as well. Again, though I can't explain everything that happened to me in that moment, I can honestly say that I became a changed man after that time.

Up until then I had always taken worship seriously, but after this time of deliverance, the feel and depth of my worship changed. A passionately intense desire for the presence of God rose up within me that was beyond what I had previously experienced. My emotions had been supernaturally enhanced by the touch of God. Tears flowed freely as I could more fully comprehend the personal agony Jesus experienced for me due to my sin. Amazingly though, I was also able to joyfully worship with a smile on my face that felt very natural and good. I wasn't smiling because it was the nice and "Christian" thing to do, but rather because I was truly enjoying worshipping the One who created me. Along with many other things, my emotions had truly been set free.

ASKING FOR BREAKTHROUGH

After going through deliverance, the intimacy I felt in my relationship with God seemed to be improved, but in some ways I still felt an invisible barrier preventing me from truly connecting in the love relationship I knew God wanted to have with me. The exciting thing was that I could finally see God, even feel Him at times through the barrier. He was becoming progressively more real to me as I continued to pour out my heart to Him. The barrier I sensed between us was beginning to weaken, and I could walk in joy knowing that barrier would eventually crumble. The seed God placed in my heart years before was going to come to fruition. I sensed I was nearing the end of winter; hope for springtime was born!

After a few months, it was clear that my newfound abundant life in Christ was genuine and I had tasted and seen that the Lord was extremely good (Psalm 34:8). My relationship with Him was far more satisfying than I had ever realized. Progress was certainly real, but it was also agonizingly slow. Many brothers and sisters, as well as my pastor Bob Beaver, continued to pour into me the love, grace, truth, and power of Jesus Christ.

Every Monday morning I gathered with a group of women to pray and worship. One morning the Holy Spirit inspired Brandy Helton, the leader, to tell us, "All you have to do is ask!" This was, of course, in reference to Jesus teaching His disciples about prayer. Jesus told His disciples that if they asked for the Holy Spirit, God wouldn't give them something harmful:

So I say to you: Ask and it will be given to you; seek and you will find; knock and the door will be opened to you. For everyone who asks receives; he who seeks finds; and to him who knocks, the door will be opened.

"Which of you fathers, if your son asks for a fish, will give him a snake instead? Or if he asks for an egg, will give him a scorpion? If you then, though you are evil, know how to give good gifts to your children, how much more will your Father in heaven give the Holy Spirit to those who ask him!"

– Luke 11:9-13

I immediately recognized this was the missing piece in my own spiritual quest! I asked her to pray for me that I would be blessed with the ability to speak in other tongues, as I had read of so many times throughout the Scriptures. The whole group prayed faithfully and passionately with me that morning. Although I was still too blocked to speak in other tongues, I experienced a deep sense of love from God, flowing through all of them and pouring into my heart – filling me with faith that someday my tongue would be freed to receive this heavenly language from the Holy Spirit as I pour out my heart "with groans that words cannot express" (Romans 8:26).

During October, Brandy began a seven-week series of classes entitled, "Who I am in Christ." She taught of God's astounding love for us, His desire for the Holy Spirit to constantly rest upon us, the authority we have in Christ, and the glorious destiny to which we are called. Her teaching was a source of great refreshment for my heart and spirit. Much of the subject matter was nothing new, but her talks were full of truth, life, passion, and power beyond all that I had ever heard. God spoke many things into my mind and heart through Brandy those weeks as she taught us about our identity in Christ. A shift was coming which would forever alter the course of my life.

The last night of the series Bob and Brandy offered prayer ministry with impartation of the Spirit to all who desired these things. My mind did not wish to participate in this even though God was drawing my heart. I could sense the spirit of antichrist wanting to hold me back from the blessing God had for me. I had never been so acutely aware of this before. Somehow I was empowered to push through this resistance in spite of my feelings. Bob and Brandy prayed into me the breaker anointing from Micah 2:13. It would be an anointing to be able to push and break through into all that God had for me. Micah said, "One who breaks open the way will go up before them; they will break through the gate and go out. Their king will pass through before them, the Lord at their head" (Micah 2:13). To be honest, I felt no breakthrough from their prayers that night, but the stage was being set for a powerful breakthrough that was about to take place in my life. The Breaker was preparing to manifest His power and His glory in a way I will never forget.

Two nights later, for the first time in my life, I was awakened by a short but intense dream that I felt was from God. Years ago I had seen a basketball hoop in the gymnasium of a very legalistic church. It was blocked by a piece of plywood that was held in place on top of the hoop by a padlocked chain. Sadly, the plywood had been secured in this way to keep neighborhood children from playing basketball in the church facility. Apparently the children had caused some sort of inconvenience to the church staff.

In my dream I again saw the basketball hoop in that church gymnasium. It was exactly as I had seen it years before. Suddenly, the chains began to crumble and fall to the ground as the piece of plywood blocking the hoop began to float up into the air. In a few seconds it was completely out of view. In a beautiful and dramatic fashion God was prophetically telling me that the Breaker (Micah

2:13) was coming. This powerful anointing of God's presence for breakthrough would soon lift what had blocked me for years. Winter was passing and springtime would soon come. Unfortunately, at the time I had no clue what this prophetic dream foretold.

Three days after the dream, Linda and I went to Dallas, Texas, to attend a large Christian conference of believers from around the world sponsored by Stand Firm World Ministries. *Texas Ablaze* is hosted in multiple cities in Texas each year by Keith and Janet Miller, a godly couple whose ministry embraces and demonstrates the glorious power of God. The theme that year was "Unlimited Anointing." Our plan was to enjoy three days of teaching, worship, and praise. It was also going to be half a week of "couple time" with my most precious and beautiful wife. How could this be anything but fun, amazing, and wonderful?

I willingly went with Linda, hoping we could both grow in the Lord while at the same time growing closer together. "Good stuff! Let's do it!" we said. I believed we would likely get some extra anointing from God while we attended. Of course we could use more; we all could! The theme of "Unlimited Anointing" sounded a bit exaggerated, even grandiose to me. I just didn't get it. The whole thing was beyond my understanding. I was about to learn a lesson straight out of Proverbs 3 - a lesson of trust.

Chapter Four

TEXAS ABLAZE:

OUR JOURNEY INTO SUPERNATURAL ENCOUNTERS WITH GOD

Linda and I both decided it was a very good idea to go to *Texas Ablaze* to grow in our relationship with God. We knew by being gone for a three-day period by ourselves, we would also have ample time to spend with each other. We weren't sure exactly what God had in store for the both of us, but He obviously knew.

Allow me to share with you my personal journal, filled with very intimate details, so you can witness the progression of our personal entry into the things of the supernatural. It was something new to us, something we were not going to be able to rely on our own understanding to comprehend. Rather, we would have to lean completely and solely upon Him.

> Trust in the Lord with all your heart and lean not on your own understanding; in all your ways acknowledge him, and he will make your paths straight.   – Proverbs 3:5-6

November 26 – Linda and I had just returned from the first evening of the conference. It was good – filled with interesting music and a passionate talk by Robert Stearns. He spoke on "God is Building a House" based on 1 Chronicles 12:32. During this time Israel was in the midst of change and was transitioning from the failed house of Saul to the blessed house of David. Even though they were in a season of transition, the sons of Issachar "understood the times" and "knew what Israel should do." As I heard him teach about this, my heart ached to leave Saul's legacy and become a "man after [God's] own heart" like David (1 Samuel 13:14).

Afterthoughts: This message and corresponding ache in my soul began to prepare my heart for what God was about to do over the next few days.

November 27 – **Morning Session:** Patricia King taught on "The Power of Expectation." She said we need a hope within us that is way beyond just wishing for something. Hope is a violent, unstoppable expectation that becomes the springboard to faith. We can only have faith for the things we hope for. That is why the writer of Hebrews defines faith as "being sure of what we hope for and certain of what we do not see" (11:1). This teaching makes me realize I need to dream big with God and persist in acting upon that dream God placed in my heart.

Afterthoughts: I didn't realize it yet, but my hope was becoming real. I was realizing my need for my hope to go from merely wishing for God to do something to an unstoppable expectation that my faith could be launched from. My expectations would soon be fulfilled far beyond what I asked for or imagined (Ephesians 3:20).

Evening Session: Bill Johnson spoke on the subject of royalty. One of the main points that stood out to me throughout his message was that servants are concerned about obedience while friends are focused on not disappointing.

Afterthoughts: This elated me because from it I knew I had become a friend of God. Obedience came more naturally to me now than it had previously. Yet, I was despondent, knowing that too often I disappointed my dearest friend.

The rest of that night I was not able to worship well. The music seemed too loud for my ears and shouts of joyful praise shocked my senses and seemed to confuse my mind. An intense spiritual battle was unfolding around and within me. I needed, but did not yet have, a violent, unstoppable expectation concerning intimacy with God. How could I sincerely hope while there was a strong, yet invisible barrier between me and the source of all true hope?

November 28 – Morning Session: I saw a middle-aged woman dancing ballet style to the praise music that was being played from the worship band. Her dancing was a graceful and beautiful expression of love to God. I have sensed off and on for about a year that I am being asked to dance before the Lord like David did (2 Samuel 6:14). There have been many excuses for not doing what the Spirit of God has asked me to do. But today the strength of these excuses weakened! I grabbed Linda and we danced together in praise to our Savior. What a beautiful time full of joy – a new way for us to express our love to God with exuberance!

During the message, Patricia King reminded us from Colossians 3:1 that we must "set [our] hearts on things above, where Christ is seated at the right hand of God." Things above are spiritual in nature, not purely intellectual. Setting our hearts and minds on things above is not done in the realm of the mind, but in the realm of the Spirit. "Things above" are in the realm of the supernatural and can only be grasped by our spirits. Only true seekers will find these things. The things of the Spirit are often packaged in a way that seems offensive to the natural mind.

Afterthoughts: I had spent much of my life in a fruitless intellectual search for a love relationship with God. Yet I knew the only way to truly connect with Him was spirit to Spirit. It all seemed so simple, but at the same time it seemed impossibly hard.

Afternoon Session: Bill Johnson warned us not to bring Scripture down to our realm of experience. He said, "If you can comprehend it, you've got a God who looks a lot like you." He also said, "The key to staying encouraged is to see and hear what God is doing now. If you are unable to do this, then remember what He has done in the past and reactivate that seed." We must never focus on what He has not done or our previous disappointments, because this increases unbelief while also increasing offense towards God. We were admonished to focus on what God was and is doing, and as we focus on that, our seed of faith and expectancy begins to grow and increase.

At the end of his message, Bill asked anyone who had not yet spoken in tongues to stand to their feet. As Linda and I stood, we were surprised to be among only ten people standing within a gathering of about five hundred. People seated near us were told to lay hands on us and pray for the receiving of the gift of the Holy Spirit. Our attempts proved to be futile; my lips were sealed as if stuck together with superglue. I could hardly utter a sound. I am confident this gift is available to many people, but I wonder if perhaps it just isn't meant for me.

Afterthoughts: That afternoon I felt weak, distant from God, and very frustrated. It was difficult to not take offense at God in my disappointment. I felt like a failure.

Evening Session: The session was good, but I did not connect well with the speaker and received little from the worship and teaching. Mahesh Chavda spoke on "The spirit of antichrist vs. the Spirit of Jesus." He said, "No demonic form can stay in the realm where the Spirit of Jesus lives, for there the impossible becomes possible."

Afterthoughts: Now I realize I was so full of the spirit of antichrist I hardly heard a great message.

I am going to stray from my journal now and simply share what happened the rest of that night and the events that followed the next day.

After he finished speaking, Mahesh imparted the Spirit of God to many people through the laying on of hands. Linda and I both went forward to receive this. Linda was eager while I was hesitant and felt doubt. She was overwhelmed by the Holy Spirit and lay peacefully at my feet. Wanting her to receive as much of God's blessing as possible, I placed my hand on her forehead and prayed as passionately as I knew how. When she sat up a few minutes later, she strongly felt the sweet love of God and yet, moments later, experienced profound grief. She cried in my arms for several minutes and then we went back to our room.

Her emotions displayed exactly what I was experiencing, a deadly serious struggle between the Spirit of Jesus and the spirit of antichrist. The battle raged within me for absolute control of my body, soul, and spirit.

A RUDE AWAKENING

That night I slept soundly – until I awoke at one o'clock in the morning remembering words spoken during some of the talks that day. Mahesh had said that speaking in tongues was an elementary gift for "babies in Christ just beginning to walk with Jesus." My mind was offended by what he had said. In the night I began to wonder, "Have I tried to follow God fifty-one years and not yet gone past baby steps in my walk? Am I a spiritual failure?" Bill Johnson had made a funny joke using the phrase, "the spirit of stupid." He meant no harm, but in the night the word "stupid" seemed so applicable to me. I cried as I heard in the night, "You have the spirit of stupid!"

Waking up again, at three in the morning, I was attacked by the same thoughts I fell asleep with. This brought back memories of how I felt in the second grade when I was doing very badly in school. That year in school, and again during this night, I felt like a complete failure – stupid, weak, and defeated. The "father of lies" (John 8:44) was attacking me through my dreams. Deep in the night I wept bitterly.

The next morning I felt oppressed and overwhelmed, wondering how I could get through the day. We went to the morning session, but neither my mind nor my heart could relate to what was going on. Linda was very concerned about me. The main theme Mahesh taught us that morning was that what you believe today, you would become tomorrow. Then he asked, "So, what do you believe?" I didn't believe very much concerning my ability to connect with the power or glory of God, and I was pessimistic concerning what I might become tomorrow.

Linda and I ate a quick lunch in our room and decided to take a short nap. We were both exhausted and depressed. But she asked me if I trusted her enough for her to help deliver me from the spiritual oppression I had been feeling. We believed the words of Jesus: "And these signs will accompany those who believe: In my name they will drive out demons" (Mark 16:17). With some hesitation I gave my approval and we began. She led me through a review of forgiveness of others and of myself. We broke judgments I had recently made, and we both began to fervently pray demanding that the spirit of heaviness leave me. An upward wave of muscular contractions, sudden tears in my eyes, and tightness in my lower abdomen were followed by a renewed sense of inner peace. I asked her to help deliver me from the spirit of antichrist that I had been feeling the past few days, which was making me want to reject and not connect with anything that was being said. Linda was not aware this was present, but I was certain it had been there all along. As we continued to pray, the same bodily responses occurred, again followed by a profound peace. Finally we told the lying spirit, which had spoken to me so strongly the night before, to leave. It was quickly gone and I felt an intense sense of relief.

Feeling the authority of Christ rising up in me, I told Linda it was time for me, in the same manner, to pray for her. At first she was surprised, but quickly sensed this was true, and agreed. As I proclaimed the lordship of Jesus and stated that all demons must flee, I touched my right hand to her forehead. Her head extended back and her body arched forward as we both sensed the powerful presence of the Holy Spirit. After several strong exhalations in the next few minutes, she suddenly relaxed, completely calm and at peace. We had both been through deliverance months before, but that day, as one flesh, we each experienced a dramatic extension of our freedom from Satan's oppression and control. A few minutes earlier we were exhausted and felt like we couldn't go on. Now, without taking that nap, we were fully refreshed and filled with a deep sense of joy. Deep within us we felt a profound peace that we were confident would never leave us again.

Minutes later, as we returned to the conference, the heaviness was completely gone. Similar to the curtain of the temple the day Jesus died on the cross (Matthew 27:51), the invisible barrier in my spiritual life was dramatically being torn in two. I could freely participate in worship with joyful exuberance, and the hope within me was rapidly rising.

BREAKTHROUGH!

That afternoon, Patricia King spoke concerning "The Mysteries of God." She said we must choose not to judge what we don't understand. Mysteries are not meant to be easily understood by the human mind, but they are only understood as the Spirit of God reveals them to our hearts. Jesus said, "Seek and you will find" (Luke 11:9), while the author of Hebrews reminds us, "[God] rewards those who earnestly seek him" (11:6). Jesus goes on to tell us that only true seekers will be allowed to understand the mysteries of God. When questioned by His disciples as to what the parables meant, He responded by saying, "The secret of the kingdom of God has been given to you. But to those on the outside everything is said in parables so that, "'They may be ever seeing but never perceiving, and ever hearing but never understanding; otherwise they might turn and be forgiven!'" (Mark 4:11-12). Needless to say, I was nearly overwhelmed by what God had already revealed to us that day. But, not known to me, there was still much more to come.

When Patricia was done speaking, she asked anyone who had not yet spoken in tongues to stand. Linda and I looked at each other and reluctantly stood again. Then she told the dozen or so of us standing to come to the front. Willingly, but with some hesitation, Linda and I walked to the stage with the others. She spoke to us for several minutes with kind and reassuring words. She communicated truth to us with gentleness and love. Our confidence grew as we listened to her and trusted in God. Patricia then said, "On the count of three, we will all start speaking in tongues ... one ... two ... three!" Linda and I opened our mouths and the Spirit of God loosed our lips. Finally, again together as one flesh, we prayed in tongues for the first time! The invisible barrier was falling to pieces.

In the evening session Bill Johnson taught that unbelief cannot exist in the presence of God's glory. Linda and I were experiencing His presence and glory in a way that we never had before, as unbelief was being pushed aside and replaced by faith. He said, "One miracle destroys ten years of bad theology." Two miracles that day had already corrected fifty years of my poor theology!

Later he had us lay hands on and pray for the healing of people suffering from various infirmities and diseases. Many reported the resolution of long-term pain and suffering. The children were asked to pray for a man near us with multiple problems. He was not healed, but one of the children praying for him received the healing. We had been noticing this particular ten-year-old girl for three days now. As she walked back from the man barefooted, she suddenly became quite excited. We saw that a plantar wart had fallen out of her foot after bothering her for six years! The healer became the healed that day. As we observed yet another miracle, our faith continued to increase.

FIRE TUNNEL

Finally that night we were all given the opportunity to pass through a spiritual gauntlet called the "fire tunnel." Each of us wrote prayer requests on a piece of paper and carried them with us through a long double line of believers praying with us for these requests and for special anointing to be imparted to us by the Holy Spirit. In addition to my written request of freedom for Christians in North Korea and China, I joyfully praised God and asked for the gifts of healing and prophecy.

As I entered the fire tunnel I could sense the invisible barrier that had plagued me for so many years no longer existed in my relationship with God. It was much like my dream a few days earlier when the chains were broken off and the plywood floated off the basketball hoop it had covered and blocked. There seemed to be nothing between my God and me any longer. His powerful presence was around me, upon me, and within me. I might have resisted, but had absolutely no desire to do so. I had already resisted far too long and I just didn't see the point of it any longer.

The weight of God's glory made me unable to stand as I received prayer and impartation. As I involuntarily leaned far to the right, three men caught me and dragged me off to the side. I was dazed but remember them saying, "This one's a heavy dragger!" Linda had made me go ahead of her, because somehow she knew this would happen and she wanted to enjoy watching me go down. I lay completely motionless for many minutes and as I slowly became more aware of consciousness, I alternated between a joy-filled, contented laughter and the tangible experience of God's amazing love giving me indescribable peace.

Out of His great kindness, God had allowed me to feel the width, depth, vastness, richness, and power of His limitless love. It was as if Paul's prayer for the Ephesians was being answered in my heart and life: "And I pray that you, being rooted and established in love, may have power, together with all the saints, to grasp how wide and long and high and deep is the love of Christ, and to know this love that surpasses knowledge – that you may be filled to the measure of all the fullness of God" (Ephesians 3:17-19). I had known of this in my mind for decades, but had never experienced His pure and intimate love in my flesh. I had read this Scripture for years, but never felt it on a level that I was feeling it that day.

His peace passed the limits of my "understanding" (Philippians 4:7). The quality and quantity of His love was greater than I could comprehend, much less put into words of description.

My human mind had been undone as my spiritual inner self was changed, renewed, and transformed by the glory of God. My spirit had been His for many years. But now my body and soul could respond in eternal harmony with His Spirit that lives within me, forever.

EXPERIENCING GOD AS ONE FLESH

Together, as one flesh, Linda and I experienced the tangible presence of God: His joy, His peace, His love, His power, and His glory. He revealed Himself to us in ways that cannot and will not be forgotten. His perfect love cast out all our fear. The Spirit of Jesus had broken through the barriers that Satan used for so many years to block our intimacy with God. We became more fully committed to a love relationship with Him that will have no end. "The secret things belong to the Lord our God, but the things revealed belong to us and to our children forever, that we may follow all the words of this law" (Deuteronomy 29:29). We were truly beginning to walk in the things that were revealed to us.

The events of that day brought about a radical shift at the very core of our relationship with Him and, ultimately, with one another. All things became new (Revelation 21:5). God had imparted to us physical manifestations and revelatory understanding of things that previously had been hidden from us. By revealing some of His secret things to us, together as one flesh God transferred us and our marriage out of the natural realm and into the realm of the supernatural. Winter had passed and the springtime had come. "See! The winter is past; the rains are over and gone. Flowers appear on the earth; the season of singing has come, the cooing of doves is heard in our land" (Song of Solomon 2:11-12). It was a glorious day! But, how does a couple get there? Where does it all begin? For us it had started years before...

Chapter Five

YOU CAN'T GET THERE FROM HERE!

A few years ago Linda and I spent ten weeks in central Maine while I attended some courses related to my field of practice, ophthalmology. Summer was the ideal time to be in this beautiful state and we delighted in the clambakes, tranquil lakes, and wild blueberries. On the weekends we would often go on short trips to other towns to enjoy the Atlantic coast ambiance while eating our fill of famous Maine lobster.

One Friday we set off for the coastal community of Camden. Somewhat confused as to the best route to use, we stopped and talked to a police officer in Waterville, which is about fifty miles from our destination. When we asked how to get to Camden, he replied with apparent seriousness, "You can't get there from here." After a brief hesitation and a wry smile from the corner of his mouth, he kindly gave us everything we needed to help us reach our destination on the rocky seashore of Maine.

For years the supernatural realm was a destination Linda and I desired to reach, yet we had no clue as to how we could start moving toward our goal. Like us, most of our Christian friends did not know how to connect with the astounding glory of God either. They believed it existed, but were not sure it was possible to experience God's glory before finally entering heaven. So often it was as if we were being told, "You can't get there from here." Unfortunately, unlike our exchange with the policeman, the initial discouraging response of a friend often became their final word on the subject. Typically, there was no helpful advice to follow.

For most of our lives Linda and I had been taught that signs and miracles accomplished through the power of God's Holy Spirit ceased with the death of the last biblical apostle, and that this supernatural activity would not be re-established until the time of Jesus' return. What our friends and mentors told us during those years was based on their interpretation of present reality. None of us had personally witnessed miraculous signs and wonders such as the believers filled with the Holy Spirit in Acts performed. After intense persecution, those empowered disciples prayed: "Stretch out your hand to heal and perform miraculous signs and wonders through the name of your holy servant Jesus" (Acts 4:30).

On the other hand, we knew the God we served had done marvelous things throughout the Old and New Testaments. And we knew many more wonders would be seen during the end times and are to be experienced by all believers forever in the New Jerusalem. It just didn't make sense to either of us that God would have avoided interacting in miraculous ways with His loved children for the past two thousand years.

Over time we came to believe with increasing certainty the promise from Micah 7:15 – God desired to show us His wonders just as He had shown them to the Israelites as they came out of

Egypt. Micah prophesied of a time when God would pour out His miraculous presence in a very tangible and significant way. He declared, "As in the days when you came out of Egypt, I will show them my wonders" (7:15).

When Linda and I pledged to each other on our twenty-fifth wedding anniversary that we were ready to "go for it," we were agreeing to pursue together increased spiritual intimacy with God. Just as when we asked the police officer in Maine how to get to Camden, we were confident the goal of spiritual connectedness with God was real and attainable. When we asked God for directions into the supernatural realm, I like to believe He delayed giving us a direct answer just long enough for us to demonstrate that our commitment was genuine. Then, with a wry smile from the corner of His mouth, He fully answered our questions. In fact, He graciously gave us more than we asked for or even imagined (Ephesians 3:20). He experientially showed us that we really could get to the realm of supernatural living from where we were. But to get started toward a supernatural goal we had to ask for supernatural help.

I want to share with you how *you* can get started in increased intimacy with God. He revealed to us the three primary ways to get started toward our supernatural goal: always **be asking**, always **be hopeful**, and **be ever ready and expectant** – because with God, anything can happen at any moment!

BE ASKING!

In the past I had asked God for many things, both in the natural and supernatural realms. Many times my requests were ineffective because I lacked the confidence that He really cared to listen. Often my prayers seemed to go no further than the walls and ceiling that surrounded me. On some occasions my petitions to God were weak because, foolishly, I was not certain I would like His answers. The problem was that I really did not know God in a real and intimate way. Sure, I knew *about* God, but didn't really *know* Him. I always said "In Jesus' name" as part of my prayers, but had never truly asked for anything in His name the way He told the disciples to ask before He returned to the Father. Jesus said to them, "Until now you have not asked for anything in my name. Ask and you will receive, and your joy will be complete" (John 16:24). Jesus was teaching His disciples to ask for things in His name and He would give them the answer they desired. If they didn't ask, there would be no answer.

This kind of asking is built upon absolute confidence that God hears our prayers. John writes in one of his letters, "This is the confidence we have in approaching God: that if we ask anything according to his will, he hears us. And if we know that he hears us – whatever we ask – we know that we have what we asked of him" (1 John 5:14-15). We also must ask with complete trust that the plans He has established for us are good and not evil (Jeremiah 29:11). Eventually I reached the point where I could boldly ask God for anything without having any concern for what His response might be. Even before I had felt the tangible touch of God's love, I knew in my heart it was real. In faith I trusted that soon His perfect love would destroy every trace of fear in my heart because "there is no fear in love" and "perfect love drives out fear, because fear has to do with punishment" (1 John 4:18). Surely God would fulfill the desires He had placed in my heart. I knew with certainty I would receive what I asked for and my joy would be complete.

KEEP ASKING

Jesus said:

Ask and it will be given to you; seek and you will find; knock and the door will be opened to you. For everyone who asks receives; he who seeks finds; and to him who knocks, the door will be opened.

Which of you, if his son asks for bread, will give him a stone? Or if he asks for a fish, will give him a snake? If you, then, though you are evil, know how to give good gifts to your children, how much more will your Father in heaven give good gifts to those who ask him!   – Matthew 7:7-11

Bill Johnson compares our search for intimacy with God to a child on an Easter egg hunt. Parents lovingly hide the colorful eggs in a way appropriate for the age of the child. The ideal hunt is one with some degree of difficulty for the hunter, yet eventual discovery is assured if the child is willing to pursue the prize. Some effort expended in the search makes the candy gained all the more sweet.

Similarly, God's presence and gifts are not hidden *from* us, but they are hidden *for* us. With wisdom God sets the degree of difficulty for our discovering Him and His blessings at exactly the right level. The writer of Proverbs says, "It is the glory of God to conceal a matter; to search out a matter is the glory of kings" (25:2). God hides Himself *for* us to pursue Him and to find Him. He is anxious to give good gifts to those who ask Him. Still, He knows our faith and commitment grow stronger as we determinedly push through the appropriate degree of resistance to get the prize we are seeking. Joy is maximized when the God-given goals of our life are met through a Spirit-led process of discovery.

This way of looking at Matthew 7 is supported by the choice of words Jesus uses in the text. The verbs chosen by Jesus and recorded by Matthew in verse 7 for *ask, seek,* and *knock* are all written in the continuous-present tense. This denotes a continuing process. This verse could be accurately translated into modern language as Kenneth Wuest has done in his translation of the New Testament:

> Keep on asking for something to be given and it shall be given you. Keep on seeking, and you shall find. Keep on reverently knocking, and it shall be opened to you. For everyone who keeps on asking for something to be given, keeps on receiving. And he who keeps on seeking, keeps on finding. And to him who keeps on reverently knocking, it shall be opened.[3]

The timing of God's answers to our prayers is always perfect, but it may not mesh well with our impatient human expectations. When we ask for spiritual gifts from God it is important that we trust Him to decide both which gifts to give us and the best timing for our receiving each gift.

In the phrase "Ask and it will be given to you," the word translated as "given" is written in the passive tense. This is significant because it implies that what we receive does not depend in any way on our labor or our striving. We are instructed to ask, yet there is no effort required to fully receive the answer. We are instructed to only ask and the rest is up to Him. Many people believe that the more they ask, the more it will be given to them. But the fact is that sometimes, if they are not careful, their asking becomes a *work* they are trying to perform in order to get Jesus to do what they are asking on their behalf.

At times we have a tendency to focus too intently on what we are asking for, forgetting our primary purpose of loving the One whom we are asking. "Overdone" asking can drift into self-centered pleading. It is possible to become so intent on requesting

---

[3]Kenneth S. Wuest, *The New Testament: An Expanded Translation*, Mt 7:7 (Grand Rapids, MI: Eerdmans, 1997, c1961). *The New American Standard Bible: 1995 Update*, (Lahabra, CA: The Lockman Foundation, 1995), also reflects this usage in the footnotes of the words "ask," "seek," and "knock" in the text.

that we forget to actually listen for God's response. Although it is good to ask and keep on asking, we must stop at times to be still and realize He has everything under control and only He is God (Psalm 46:10). We also must learn to stop asking for long enough to listen for the response of God (1 Kings 19:12). This can only be done with the ears He gives us to hear (Mark 4:9). We must desire to hear, take time to be still, and be willing to listen to what He has to say – even if the response, or the timing of the response, is not what we would plan.

His Ways and Thoughts Are Different

Isaiah reminds us that God's ways and our ways are not the same. God says through him: "'For my thoughts are not your thoughts, neither are your ways my ways,' declares the Lord. 'As the heavens are higher than the earth, so are my ways higher than your ways and my thoughts than your thoughts'" (Isaiah 55:8-9). His ways and thoughts are on a level far beyond our human capacity and His wisdom greatly exceeds what we have access to in the natural realm.

Fortunately, He chooses to share with us the wisdom and glory of the supernatural realm. For Isaiah goes on to declare that, "As the rain and snow come down from heaven, and do not return to it without watering the earth and making it bud and flourish, so that it yields seed for the sower and bread for the eater, so is my word that goes out from my mouth: It will not return to me empty, but will accomplish what I desire and achieve the purpose for which I sent it" (Isaiah 55:10-11). Just as the rain and snow come from heaven, so God is able to share His thoughts with us through the supernatural realm.

The direct leading of God will always surprise as well as bless us. His ways are always prosperous (Psalm 10:5) and we must not react to a response from God by rejecting what He intends for us to receive. Jesus always did exactly what the Father commanded Him to do (John 14:31) and said just what the Father told Him to say (John 12:50). It is essential that we learn to do the same.

God has initiated an intimate love relationship with each one of us. He has placed within us an insatiable desire for His love and a deep yearning for the glorious things of heaven. It honors Him greatly when we ask Him to supernaturally satisfy our needs. When we keep on asking, seeking, and knocking, God promises that He will supply exactly what we need for life and godliness (2 Peter 1:3). We can absolutely and unconditionally trust this promise that He will supply us with all we need to live a holy life in a supernatural way.

BE HOPEFUL

Last summer, Linda and I spent a week on a Caribbean island called Saint Maarten to rest and also work on this book. The condominium we stayed in had a very large window which provided a magnificent view of the aqua blue sea surrounding our small island. It was one of the most beautiful places I've ever seen.

During our fifth day on Saint Maarten, there was a change in the weather. A hurricane was passing by four hundred miles to the north, altering the humidity of the air. Although the sky remained blue, as it had been each day before, something in the atmosphere had changed. Suddenly we noticed a large mountain, perfectly centered in the view of the Caribbean Sea from our room. What we saw turned out to be a five-square-mile volcanic island called Saba with peaks reaching nearly three thousand feet above sea level. Saba Island was huge and undeniably real, yet it remained undetected in the center of our condominium view for five days. The weather that day looked exactly the same as before, but our view was strikingly different.

An hour later we detected a second island, Saint Eustatius, further in the distance to the southwest of Saba. As the day passed, both islands gradually disappeared into the misty horizon over the crystal clear sea. Neither could then be seen when the higher humidity was present, yet the experience of seeing the mountain earlier that day left us with knowledge and confidence of the reality of each island. After becoming aware of their existence, we knew it was likely that we would see this sight again.

The next day the mountain of Saba reappeared, just as we had expected. But its outline was so faint it would have gone unnoticed had we not been intently looking for it. The island was just as large as the day before, yet could easily have gone undetected had we not hoped to see it again. Although we searched for a glimpse of Saint Eustatius, it did not reappear that day, yet we knew of its very real existence. Due to the experience we had the day before, both Linda and I took great pleasure in looking for them and perceiving them whenever possible.

The supernatural component of our marriage was much like these islands for twenty-five years. Intimate connectedness with the Holy Spirit was right in front of us ready to be perceived, but we didn't know where to look or even what we were looking for! As the weather conditions obscured the islands for days, so our spiritual condition was not yet right for us to be allowed experiential access to the realm of God's glory. When hope had grown strong within each of us, we asked God to reveal Himself to us in the supernatural realm. He miraculously opened our blind spiritual eyes and softened our hearts of stone (Ephesians 2:1-10; Ezekiel 36:26). God allowed each of us to experience His glorious presence which for so long had been hidden *for* us, not *from* us, as we had previously thought.

Encountering God through Hope

Encountering God is very similar to the way we observed the islands those days in Saint Maarten. Initially, we were overwhelmed by the sudden and obvious way God revealed Himself to us. Soon we discovered God had another aspect of His glory to show us, and then still another. Our God has no limitations, so there is always more that can be experienced with Him. Yet sometimes His presence is seemingly obscured. At other times it can be difficult to strongly encounter His glory. During these times, though, it is extremely valuable for us to know from past experience how completely real God is, where to look for Him, and how to find Him again. It is good to remember that God is "not far from each one of us" (Acts 17:27).

The supernatural realm is a reality that God planned to make available to us before we were consciously aware of it. Once we experienced the tangible presence of God, there was no longer any doubt concerning His existence or His accessibility in that realm. I had the privilege of spending two hours with Peter Lord in an airport a few years ago. He told me something I will never forget. Peter said, "A man with an experience is never at the mercy of a man with an argument." At the time, I only partially understood what he meant. Once I personally experienced the astounding glory of God, his statement made complete sense to my mind as well as my heart. I didn't understand what he was talking about at first because I lacked the experience with God that I needed. But once I had encountered God in ways I never had previously, his statement made perfect sense to me.

Although we were neither fully sure of what we hoped for, nor completely certain of what we had not yet seen (Hebrew 11:1), God allowed both Linda and me to experience the manifest presence of Holy God. No one can possibly convince us that God does not exist, not because we read about Him but because we have experienced Him! Our faith in Him is sure and it is everlasting. He has shared His eternal glory with us as His children, allowing us to sense His supernatural essence in our natural flesh. We are not unique in our ability to be transformed by the glory of God. In fact, any believer who is asking and hopeful can be filled with the Holy Spirit, who ushers us into the supernatural realm of God's Kingdom. It is only through the presence of God's Holy Spirit in us that we can fulfill the destiny to which we have been called.

Fulfilling Our Destiny through Hope

It really helps us to know where God wants us to go in life. The major purpose of this book is to communicate throughout the kingdom the revelation of marriage being lived out in the realm of the supernatural. God wants believers to recognize His ultimate plan for what marriage is meant to be. When two individuals, as one flesh in marital union, are consistently filled with the glorious presence of God's Spirit, they are enabled to function with supernatural wisdom, understanding, and authority. Their marriage and ministry exit the restraints of the natural world, allowing them to do wonderful things that can only be accomplished through the counsel and might of God. This kind of marital partnership changes the world and advances His Kingdom. It also brings great honor to the King of kings and the Lord of lords.

God wants believers to recognize the ultimate plan of what He desires marriage to be. The hope God places within us for marriage is not that it be pretty good, normal, or even acceptable. Hope from God is a supernatural destiny that far exceeds the ordinary plans of men. Heaven-inspired hope goes way beyond standard human expectations. God-given goals are extraordinary and cannot be reached without supernatural intervention. Thankfully, He is willing and able to help us reach the destiny placed before us in our marriages. We have been promised that hope will not disappoint us, as Paul wrote to the Romans: "And hope does not disappoint us, because God has poured out his love into our hearts by the Holy Spirit, whom he has given us" (Romans 5:5).

Secure Hope that Prospers

What I speak of is not a naïve hope. God passionately loves marriage and it plays a central role in His biblical presentation of creation (Genesis 1-2), redemption (Ephesians 5:22-33), and the triumphant return of Christ (Revelation 19:6-10). Our fulfilling the true plan of marriage is vitally important to God. He is strongly motivated to propel each marital couple into the full destiny for which their union was created. Supernatural marriage is a rich and secure relationship which validates God's promise to share with us His secret things that they may belong to us and to our children forever. God promises us through Moses: "The secret things belong to the Lord our God, but the things revealed belong to us and to our children forever, that we may follow all the words of this law" (Deuteronomy 29:29).

Every married believer should hold on tenaciously to the real hope of functioning within the supernatural realm in marriage. Ideally both spouses share this hope, but even an unequally yoked partner can receive this eternal blessing.[4] Intimate relationship with God always brings rich blessings to us and increased glory to our King. The pursuit and participation of even one spouse in supernatural marriage prophetically points to the culmination of God's plan for the church when she is finally united as the perfect supernatural bride of Christ.

---

[4]For helpful ways to live in an unequally yoked marriage, see "Addendum" at the end of the book: "Advice to Laura: How to Live When Unequally Yoked."

Our hope to experience supernatural marriage is real. Hope is a seed planted in our spirit by God and we know that true hope only comes from Him, as David says in Psalm 62:5: "Find rest, O my soul, in God alone; my hope comes from him." From the seed of hope sprouts joyful expectancy as we boldly anticipate what is to come: "Therefore, since we have such a hope, we are very bold" (2 Corinthians 3:12). The new growth of hope is watered by faith, and it is through faith that we become "sure of what we hope for and certain of what we do not see" (Hebrews 11:1). Through the help of the Holy Spirit we wait patiently for what we hope for, but do not yet have: "But if we hope for what we do not yet have, we wait for it patiently" (Romans 8:25).

The Lord further declares through Jeremiah, the plans and the hope He has for us:

> "For I know the plans I have for you," declares the Lord, "plans to prosper you and not to harm you, plans to give you hope and a future. Then you will call upon me and come and pray to me, and I will listen to you. You will seek me and find me when you seek me with all your heart. I will be found by you," declares the Lord.   – Jeremiah 29:11-14

As with every other aspect of our lives, God's plan for our marriages is to prosper them, by giving us hope and drawing us into a glorious future. When we call to God, He truly will listen and answer us. Those who seek Him with all their heart will find Him. These are promises that encourage us and lead us into our destinies. Be hopeful! Our glorious future is safe and secure in the hands of our supernatural God.

BE EVER READY AND EXPECTANT

The third step in encouraging you to get started in the pursuit of intimacy with God is to always be ready! Our God is both surprising and astonishing. He surprises us in the sudden and unexpected ways He acts. We are astounded by the magnitude and significance of what He chooses to do. In the back of my mind throughout the writing of this book has been the exhortation to be ready, because with God, big things can happen in a moment.

New Levels of Supernatural Experience

A few months ago I received a dream that continues to remind me how swiftly God accomplishes His plans and how we can best participate with Him in fulfilling them. In my dream Linda and I were in school headed toward our next class, which was located far away. Walking together, we saw a huge crane, perhaps a half of a mile in height. We stepped into a gondola, similar to those used to lift snow skiers up the mountain, which was attached to the end of the crane's cable. In less than ten seconds the gondola was effortlessly lifted high into the sky, swung across several city blocks, and gently deposited at a completely new location. Immediately we exited its door and began to scramble up an extremely tall pole, similar to the trunk of a great tree. The climbing required some effort on our part, but we proceeded with smoothness resulting in rapid ascent. Soon we were both climbing high into the thin atmosphere of the clear blue sky. At times it was frightening, but the overall emotions we felt were excitement and joy.

Through this dream God showed me several things about how we are to interact with Him if we are to advance in His glorious Kingdom. Our going to classes symbolizes the value of our desire to learn more about the ways and plans of God. When He knows we are ready, at precisely the time of His choosing, God dramatically lifts us away from where we have been in order to place us where He wants us to be. In a moment we are moved to the new place where He prefers us to be – His perfect will. This transfer from one level of glory to another occurs suddenly and requires no effort on our part. Paul said it like this in contrasting the Old Covenant with the New Covenant: "And we, who with unveiled faces all reflect the Lord's glory, are being transformed into his likeness with ever-increasing glory, which comes from the Lord, who is the Spirit" (2 Corinthians 3:18). It is a sovereign act by the King of glory. Again, with God, big things can happen in a moment.

God celebrates with us when He moves us into a new level of spiritual maturity or supernatural experience. Both He and we are filled with joy as we progress in these new realms. Our Redeemer wants us to be completely "transformed by the renewing of [our] mind" (Romans 12:2). However, after bringing us to a new level of glory, neither He nor we will be satisfied if progress does not continue. In my dream Linda and I immediately resumed our pursuit of the next higher level of glory. We must learn to be content and thankful for where we are, yet at the same time continue to press into God for more of His glory to be revealed. It is a lifelong quest that will continue until the day we die. We desire, so we ask. We hope and are made ready. God transforms us, so we are thankful. He supernaturally places desire for still more within us, and the cycle begins anew. With each turn God helps us to climb higher and higher toward heaven. Each transition into greater glory brings us closer to becoming who God created us to be. Through transformation by the Spirit of God, we, the eternally redeemed, are being made holy (Hebrews 10:14).

Although it is a complex process, I emphasize here the importance of being ready. God yearns to take every one of us "from glory to glory" (2 Corinthians 3:18, NKJV). He wants us to experience all that is available in His glorious Kingdom. Sometimes we get discouraged seeing God lavish spiritual gifts on others while we, though faithful, have not yet received what we have desired. Our Father speaks to us the same words spoken by the prodigal's father to the older, disheartened son: "My son...you are always with me, and everything I have is yours" (Luke 15:31). We can confidently trust our Father in heaven to give good gifts to those who ask Him (Matthew 7:11). When we ask, though, we must be ready, expecting to receive that for which we are asking. By faith we expect a supernatural, life-altering response to come as we cry out to God.

God's Glory Overtakes Us

God does not hold the supernatural experiences Linda and I were blessed with during the last day of the conference in Dallas in reserve for only a few special believers. They are available to all who truly desire them and ask for them. Similar to the gondola in my dream, the Holy Spirit suddenly lifts us out of the natural realm and deposits us into the astounding supernatural realm. In doing this God disrupts our normal mental and physical functions as a way of dramatically opening our spiritual eyes. He wants us to literally see His glory. The presence of His glory overwhelms our natural body systems and takes over their control. This often happens abruptly, shocking our mortal minds and physical senses. When our sensations and functions are transferred out of the natural and into the supernatural realm, they behave differently.

For example:

1. We may speak in tongues that are unintelligible to human ears.
   - "If I speak in the tongues of men and of angels..."
     – 1 Corinthians 13:1

- "And in the church God has appointed ... those speaking in different kinds of tongues."
  - 1 Corinthians 12:28
- Paul said, "I thank God that I speak in tongues more than all of you." - 1 Corinthians 14:18

2. As seen in the Bible from Genesis to Revelation, the weighty presence of God's glory can make it awkward or even impossible to stand.
   - "Abram fell facedown, and God said to him..."
     - Genesis 17:3
   - In describing the glory of God, Ezekiel said, "Like the appearance of a rainbow in the clouds on a rainy day, so was the radiance around him. This was the appearance of the likeness of the glory of the Lord. When I saw it, I fell facedown, and I heard the voice of the one speaking." - Ezekiel 1:28
   - "When Jesus said, 'I am he,' they drew back and fell to the ground." - John 18:6
   - In describing his vision of Jesus, John said, "When I saw him, I fell at his feet as though dead."
     - Revelation 1:17

3. Words of knowledge are given supernaturally to believers for their work in the Kingdom.
   - "Now about spiritual gifts ... the manifestation of the Spirit is given for the common good. To one there is given ... the message of knowledge by means of the same Spirit." - 1 Corinthians 12:1, 7-8
   - "Then Peter said, 'Ananias, how is it that Satan has so filled your heart that you have lied to the Holy Spirit and have kept for yourself some the money you received for the land?'" - Acts 5:3, Acts 5:1-11

4.   Spiritual dreams.
   • Jacob "had a dream in which he saw a stairway resting on the earth, with its top reaching to heaven, and the angels of God were ascending and descending on it." – Genesis 28:12, see Genesis 28:10-22
   • Peter quoted Joel on the day of Pentecost and said, "In the last days, God says, I will pour out my Spirit on all people. Your sons and daughters will prophesy, your young men will see visions, your old men will dream dreams." – Acts 2:17

5.   Prophetic declarations.
   • Numerous examples throughout the books of Isaiah and Daniel.
   • "After we had been there a number of days, a prophet named Agabus came down from Judea. Coming over to us, he took Paul's belt, tied his own hands and feet with it and said, 'The Holy Spirit says, "In this way the Jews of Jerusalem will bind the owner of this belt and will hand him over to the Gentiles."'" – Acts 21:10-11

6.   Holy travail.
   • "My dear children, for whom I am again in the pains of childbirth until Christ is formed in you." – Galatians 4:19
   • "Oh, that my head were a spring of water and my eyes a fountain of tears! I would weep day and night for the slain of my people." – Jeremiah 9:1

7.   Behavior that is considered "socially inappropriate."
   • The unbelievers on the Day of Pentecost thought the others were drunk when they were filled with

the Holy Spirit because of the way they were acting after being filled with the Spirit. Peter's response was, "These men are not drunk, as you suppose. It's only nine in the morning! No, this is what was spoken by the prophet Joel..." – Acts 2:15-16

These are but a few of the manifestations of God's presence in and upon us when He decides to visit us with His glory. When we allow the Holy Spirit to alter our thinking, emotions, and physical actions, we are permitting our natural selves to be used at God's discretion in the supernatural sphere. This will not happen unless we are willing to submit everything we have and every aspect of who we are to His sovereign control. James said, "Submit yourselves, then, to God" (James 4:7). This submission is required if we are expecting God to touch us and change us in the ways we desire.

Example of Paul

The conversion of Saul the persecutor to Paul the apostle is an excellent demonstration of how quickly and dramatically the glorious presence of God can change those who make their hearts available to Him. Saul's beliefs about Jesus, although strongly held, were completely incorrect. Yet, the desires of his heart were sincere and good because he thought he was serving God according to what he had been taught. God honored his passion, but abruptly corrected his theology through an experience which could not be ignored or misunderstood by Paul himself. On the road to Damascus, his body, soul, and spirit encountered the glorious presence of Jesus in a spectacular and unforgettable way. But there was much more required before the transformation would be complete. Physical eyes were temporarily blinded so that spiritual eyes could forever see (Acts 9:9, 11-12, 17-19).

Paul was blinded in the natural realm by the light of Jesus' supernatural glory. He and his traveling companions immediately fell down, unable to stand in the weighty presence of God. During three days of being blinded to normal human experience, Paul became acutely aware of Jesus' reality. He was completely ready to hear what God had to speak to his mind and heart. Paul's blindness in the natural domain emphasized the fact that his vision of Ananias coming to restore his sight was of supernatural origin.

In the vision, Paul was instructed to humbly submit himself to another man who intimately knew Jesus. At the time Ananias carried more spiritual authority than Paul. Through the laying on of hands Paul's physical eyes were miraculously opened. And as Ananias prayed, Paul was filled with the Holy Spirit, fully opening his spiritual eyes. In a moment he was doubly healed – both physically and spiritually. Immediately Paul went into ministry, sharing with others the glorious revelations he had received. Luke writes that, "At once he began to preach in the synagogues that Jesus is the Son of God" (Acts 9:20). From that time forward he selflessly gave himself to others and followed the leading of the Holy Spirit in every aspect of his life, just as Jesus had taught him in their supernatural encounter together.

Supernatural Realm Progressively Revealed

As believers, our transition into the supernatural realm of heaven is much the same as that of Paul, often involving an extraordinary spiritual experience or a series of strikingly real interactions with the glory of God. These encounters are thrilling and amazing. They open our blind spiritual eyes to clearly see the reality and significance of God's desire to commune with us Spirit to spirit. Intimate connectedness with the Holy Spirit changes our preconceived notions and improves our understanding of how

God desires to interact with His children. Much like God asking Job where he was when the earth was formed, we are dramatically reminded of who God is and who we are not. God said to Job: "Where were you when I laid the earth's foundation? Tell me, if you understand. Who marked off its dimensions? Surely you know!" (Job 38:4-5). Seeing, hearing, or feeling the astonishingly real presence of Holy God is meant to radically change us. After experiencing God's glory we should no longer be the same. Each experience of His glory is an opportunity to enter and dwell in the supernatural sphere.

God does not choose us to intimately relate to Him based on the correctness of our theology. Saul's initial view of Jesus was the opposite of the truth. There are many aspects of God and His Kingdom which we inadequately understand and improperly teach. Yet, God sees beyond the limitations of our mental comprehension and He looks directly into our hearts. God can easily discern the difference between those who seek to know about Him and those who desire to know Him. God is not impressed with our memorization of Scripture or our ability to win a religious debate, but He will dramatically reward those who earnestly seek Him (Hebrews 11:6).

Learning to live in the supernatural realm is not typically accomplished by one astounding event. The capacity to intimately live with the Spirit of God is not fully delivered by a single experience. But it starts as we receive our first overwhelming taste from the river of the water of life (Revelation 22:1). It will develop over time through the process of daily pursuing and accepting God's glorious presence.

Following Paul's encounter with Jesus on the road to Damascus, his way of relating to God was forever changed. The rest of his life on earth, Paul was intentionally alert, looking to receive guidance from the Holy Spirit. Sudden and unexpected supernatural events happened repeatedly throughout his ministry because he was always ready to hear the voice of God and obediently respond to everything he was told to do. The same can be true for each of us today. Be ready! Astounding things can happen in a moment.

SUMMARY

Deep within us we all have a longing to participate with God in His supernatural realm. Our desire to reach into the eternal grows from a knowing that God is absolutely real and our planned destiny is to share in His unending glory. We tenaciously hold on to the hope of intimately connecting with the Spirit of God because that hope is securely established in truth. His unchanging Word tells us that Christ is seated at the right hand of God (Ephesians 1:20) and we are seated with Him in the heavenly realms (Ephesians 2:6). Jesus says, "Where I am, my servant also will be" (John 12:26) and "Father, I want those you have given me to be with me where I am, and to see my glory" (John 17:24).

Jesus fully participated in God's supernatural realm while completely surrounded by the natural realm of this world. He often asked for help from heaven and listened intently to every response He received. Yet, it was not Jesus' spiritual position or ability to hear that most pleased His Father. The thing Jesus did that led His Father to be well pleased is the same thing which brought Him eternal glory and honor: Jesus was obedient, doing exactly what He was asked to do. If we are to live in the supernatural realm with God, we must do the same.

In the next chapter, we are going to begin our focus on establishing Jesus as the true Lord of our lives and marriages. What we receive in the supernatural realm is of inestimable potential worth. Yet, spiritual gifts will be of no eternal value unless they are used under the authority of the One who gave them. There is only one Lord in the Kingdom of light and obedience to Him is the only acceptable option. Functioning in God's supernatural realm requires a serious commitment to the lordship of Jesus Christ.

Chapter Six

SAVIOR, BUT LORD?

SALVATION AND LORDSHIP

"Where do I begin to tell the story of how great a love can be?" That opening line of the theme to the movie *Love Story* was my primary question as I began to write this book. The covenant of marriage between my wife and I has been a blessing beyond words. It has surprised us how great a love can exist between two individuals. I am passionate to share what God has taught us through our twenty-eight years of marriage at the time of this writing. I am confident that what we have learned can bring any believer encouragement, strength, and wisdom to deal more joyfully and effectively in their own marital relationship. *But the structure of a marriage which fulfills its destiny in the plans of God can only be built upon a supernatural foundation.* This is where the story must begin!

Jesus is the cornerstone in the construction of supernatural marriage (Ephesians 2:20; 1 Peter 2:6). The foundation is laid in the establishing of an intimate love relationship with our supernatural God. Only when we are in Him and He is in us (John 17:21) can we possess His perfect love. The holy love we receive from God is the driving force behind our ability to become truly one flesh in body, soul, and spirit with our marriage partner.

Establishing and maintaining an intimate love relationship with God requires the critical foundational components of salvation and lordship. The truths of salvation are extensively taught in the Evangelical church, so most Christians in these churches have a reasonably good grasp of what salvation means and how it is obtained through repentance and faith in Jesus Christ. On the other hand, true lordship is inconsistently taught and poorly understood within the church today, and rarely practiced by the individual believer. This lordship deficit is extremely damaging to the development of intimacy with God. Without Jesus truly being Lord in our individual lives and within our marriages, the potential for authentic oneness in the relationships is lost.

In discussions, sermons, and official church ceremonies Jesus is often described as our "Lord and Savior." The words "Lord" and "Savior" are spoken almost as one word. It is true that these two words are closely related, but they actually represent two quite separate aspects of our relationship with Jesus. Jesus cannot be Lord of our lives until we accept Him as our Savior. Unfortunately, our proclamation of Him as Savior often does not result in the practical reality of His being Lord in our lives.

By age eleven I had heard innumerable sermons concerning sin, hell, coming judgment, and the need for salvation through Jesus. When asked if I was ready to accept Jesus as my Lord and Savior, I said, "Yes!" Who wouldn't want to spend eternity in the bliss of heaven, avoiding eternal torture in fire? Undoubtedly, I needed to be saved from hell, but I had no clue what true lordship really meant. I just assumed lordship would, with a little effort, follow after salvation. To my surprise, it did not naturally flow out of the experience of salvation.

Linda and I have discovered through working with people in deliverance ministry that many believers share this same misconception. Some who are saved are immediately drawn into establishing Jesus as their true Lord. This smooth transition into lordship is ideal and attainable. But many claim salvation in Jesus, yet delay their true acceptance of Him as Lord for months, years – or for the remainder of their lifetimes!

I foolishly allowed years to pass through high school, college, and most of medical school before being willing to make this commitment. I now describe that time of life as "the years the locusts have eaten" (Joel 2:25). I knew Jesus was not Lord of certain areas of my life, but stubbornly put off submission to Him in those areas. It was similar to what I heard Juan Carlos Ortiz say on one occasion – we often sing with our voices the hymn "He is Lord," while whispering in our minds, "but, I am the prime minister!" My self-satisfaction and acceptance of partial obedience led to much pain and injury, both to myself and others. Satan had deceived me into settling for only a small part of the glory God made completely available to His children. For a time, I allowed goals and pleasures in the natural realm to take priority over the divine plans and commands of the God who created nature. Unfortunately, this perverse and unwise way of living is common even among those who say and sing, "Jesus is Lord!"

It is really not difficult to learn from the Bible which behaviors honor God and which are rebellion against His will. God does not hide these things from us. The Holy Spirit is also reliable in telling us when we venture into sin. In fact, one of the main reasons He came was to convict the world of sin, righteousness, and judgment

(John 16:5-11). I repeatedly ignored the promptings of the Spirit through rationalization that none of us are really expected to be perfect. Yet, God clearly tells us to "be holy" just as He is holy (Leviticus 11:44; 1 Peter 1:16). I saw holiness as a burden placed on us by a God who expected a little too much of us. I tried in my own strength to honor God in many ways, but intentionally held on to sin by being selfish, impure, and stubbornly resistant to the ways He desired to change me. The basic problem underlying my disobedience was that my love for God was very weak and I was not even close to understanding His beautiful supernatural love for me.

In my final year of medical school, my two most pressing goals were to become a doctor and to find a godly wife. Both of these goals were good in and of themselves, but the problem was the way I pursued them. My life was out of balance. I spent so much time and effort trying to find a woman to love, I hardly paid attention to developing a love relationship with God, the eternal source of all true love. As I strived on my own to find fulfillment, my dearest relationships crumbled all around me. This was specifically because those relationships were self-centered – they were all about me. It is good to seek love, but it will never be found through focus on self or the pursuit of personal satisfaction. Authentic love relationships that fulfill the destiny of marriage will not develop without a serious and consistent commitment to the lordship of Jesus. They cannot be obtained in the presence of compromise. It really must all be about Him.

God places within each of us an incredibly strong desire to receive and give love. His plan is that we would receive His perfect love, return that love to Him, and share it with all whom we encounter. This is why, when an expert in the law asked Jesus which commandment was the greatest, He responded by saying, "'Love the Lord your God with all your heart and with all your soul and with all your mind.' This is the first and greatest commandment. And the second is like it: 'Love your neighbor as yourself.' All the Law and the Prophets hang on these two commandments" (Matthew 22:37-40).

Holy love flowing through us drastically alters how we think and act. It literally transforms us – changing who we are and who we will become. This pure and effective form of love cannot be produced by effort in the natural realm. It cannot be manufactured from within our own mind or heart. Holy love can only be received as a gift from God, who supernaturally places it in our hearts.

LORDSHIP: COMPLETE OBEDIENCE MOTIVATED BY LOVE

The supernatural gift of love we receive from God has two main purposes. **The first is that it enables us to fully and freely love one another.** When we love others, it completes His love in us. What a grand opportunity to participate in this beautiful and eternal circle of love!

As partners in marriage receiving God's supernatural love, we are empowered to love one another deeply and consistently. The purpose of this love relationship is much bigger than the marriage itself. Its ultimate destiny is to complete the circle, which begins and ends within God's everlasting love. John writes, "No one has ever seen God; but if we love one another, God lives in us and his love is made complete in us" (1 John 4:12). One of the ways God's love is revealed in the earth today is through men and women submitted to His lordship and letting His love be expressed through their actions to others. Even though no one has seen God, they in a sense see Him via His love manifested in us.

The second purpose of God's gift of perfect love is to make true obedience possible. Jesus said, "If anyone loves me, he will obey my teaching. My Father will love him, and we will come to him and make our home with him" (John 14:23). Obedience is the expected result of the holy Lover taking up residence within the wholly loved. God's plans for our lives are incredibly good and He wants to prosper us, providing hope and a future (Jeremiah 29:11). His design is that we experience joy and deep satisfaction in our relationships with others, particularly in marriage. However, God's planned destiny for holy matrimony will not be realized until His perfect love dwells within each marital partner, enabling them not only to truly love one another but also to walk in authentic obedience. Voluntary obedience is the second means of completing God's love.

Through responsive obedience the eternal, self-perpetuating flow of God's love can be seen. We receive His perfect gift of love and it supernaturally leads us to accept and respond to Him as Lord. Our greatest joy becomes obeying God, because we desire to please Him. He becomes our dearest friend who restores our souls and guides us "in paths of righteousness for his name's sake" (Psalm 23:3). Joyfully obedient, we remain in His love, for His love has been made complete. "But if anyone obeys his word, God's love is truly made complete in him" (1 John 2:5). Similar to the first love circle, this cycle of love and obedience has a beginning but no intended end. God's desire is that we remain both in love with Him and obedient to Him forever.

Our love and our obedience are both responses to God's perfect love. Jesus said, "If you obey my commands, you will remain in my love, just as I have obeyed my Father's commands and remain in his love" (John 15:10). With each turn of these love-centered cycles, His glory is multiplied. When our lives and marriages revolve around perfect love, we "reflect the Lord's glory" and are "transformed into his likeness with ever-increasing glory" (2 Corinthians

3:18). Marriage empowered by God's holy love is supernatural and participates fully in the increase of His government and peace that will never end (Isaiah 9:7). Through love and obedience we share in God's glory while we actually increase His glory.

"God is love" (1 John 4:8) and He is full of glory (Habakkuk 3:3). When we receive God's holy love, we are transformed to become more like Him, empowering us to love without restraint and obey without hesitation. As we reflect the Lord's glory, His glory is forever increased. What a joy to participate in this eternal cycle of love and obedience! Again Paul writes, "And we, who with unveiled faces all reflect the Lord's glory, are being transformed into his likeness with ever-increasing glory, which comes from the Lord, who is the Spirit" (2 Corinthians 3:18).

True obedience seems far off and unobtainable when we think of it with our natural mind. But as we gaze into the loving eyes of the Father, obeying all His desires becomes normal, instinctive, and effortless. Jesus reminds us in Matthew 11:30, "My yoke is easy and my burden is light." An intimate love relationship with the Father through Jesus is what makes the burden of obedience light. We cannot fully receive God's love, individually or in a marriage, until we make the decision to pursue complete obedience and make Jesus truly Lord of our lives.

This was the stumbling block during my teen years and early twenties. I knew God desired that I fully follow His ways, yet I deliberately pursued the course of incomplete obedience. Sadly, this is a path that many believers follow. It is based in rebellion, which Samuel equated with the sin of divination as he rebuked King Saul (1 Samuel 15:23).

The patience of God allows for our imperfection, but His justice requires change in those who are deliberately disobedient. We may describe our rebellion as naughtiness or admit to others that we sometimes "slip up" or succumb to an occasional indiscretion. These euphemisms may appease our consciences, but they do nothing to limit the destructive effects of willful sin in our lives and in our marriages. God easily discerns the hearts of men and He will not be mocked. God will not freely share His love or His glory with anyone in rebellion against Him. In fact, when the Galatians were in a position of incomplete obedience, Paul warned them that their actions sown to please the sinful nature would produce destructive fruit in their lives. He said, "Do not be deceived: God cannot be mocked. A man reaps what he sows" (Galatians 6:7).

LORDSHIP: THE KEY TO INTIMACY

The decision to make Jesus fully Lord of our lives leads to receiving both the holy love of God and the ability to fully obey Him. Lordship is the key to experiencing an intimate relationship with Holy God. Isaiah prophesied that Jesus would have "the Spirit of knowledge and of the fear of the Lord" (11:2). The Spirit of knowledge allowed Jesus, and it allows us, to intimately know and appreciate God. When we really come to know God, it is inevitable that we will passionately love Him. In this passage, the Spirit of knowledge is linked to the fear of the Lord because an intimate love relationship with the Father, the Son, and the Holy Spirit will deposit in our souls the joyful and insatiable desire to respond with complete obedience. If we know God, we will love Him. And if we love God, the natural result is that we will obey Him. Again Jesus said, "If you love me, you will obey what I command" (John 14:15).

It is God's specific requirement that each individual believer is to become holy because God is holy (Leviticus 11:44). When a person's true heart desire is holiness, God will usher him into the supernatural realm. In order to develop rich intimacy within marriage, each partner must first develop genuine intimacy with Holy God. Through that divine relationship God imparts to us His perfect love, leading us into obedience and miraculously transforming us into the mature spouses, parents, and lovers He intended us to be. Only when we are individually involved in a supernatural love relationship with God is it possible to participate in a supernatural marriage.

An Important Lesson

All my life I felt intensely drawn towards marriage – even when I was a small child. God placed this desire for marriage in me for His purposes, to be used for His glory. For years I misunderstood and misapplied this yearning, seeking to satisfy its intention in the natural realm through my own perceptions and abilities; the sins of selfishness, stubbornness, and compromise were prominent in my life. In spite of my failings, God did not revoke His special plan for my marriage. My Father loves me and loves marriage with all His heart. However, He did not allow me to have this awesome gift until I had accepted Jesus' lordship over my life. Then it was released to me! Although God does not demand that this step be taken by all who enter marriage, I believe it was required in my life to teach me that God requires lordship before fulfilling the deepest desires of our hearts.

God said through Isaiah thousands of years before: "I will give you the treasures of darkness, riches stored in secret places, so that you may know that I am the Lord, the God of Israel, who summons you by name" (45:3). Unknown to me at the time, my desire for an outstanding marriage was meant to draw me into a supernatural marriage. This treasure was hidden in a secret place. God wanted it discovered and released to me and to the one who would become my wife. But the marriage I craved in my heart would never be obtainable in the natural realm alone. The treasure of supernatural marriage was hidden by darkness until it was made visible by the glorious light from God's supernatural realm.

By my senior year in medical school, the lordship of Jesus in my life was still very incomplete. Because of this, God allowed many aspects of my life to spiral downward. Outwardly my life looked like a glorious success story, but inside it was obvious I was headed for complete failure. I knew the glory of the Lord was not in me. I was badly missing the goal God had placed before me. My incomplete acceptance of Jesus' lordship had dragged me downward far too long, yet God was prepared to forever change me. Remember that with God really big things can happen in a moment.

One afternoon I fell on my face before God in complete despair. With sincerity I declared that I was incapable of being in charge of my life. I gave all control to Jesus and verbally declared Him to be Lord of all. I really had no idea what that meant or what it would look like in day-to-day life. How would this all play out? What exactly does one do when Jesus is Lord? I didn't know what to expect in the future. The important thing was that for the first time I trusted God to lead me into that future. Within my mind and heart I shouted to God the same words Samuel spoke when he heard God's voice the fourth time, "Speak, for your servant is listening" (1 Samuel 3:10). God opened my deaf ears and spoke into them. He began to teach me how to live and how to love.

Two weeks later my long struggle to find the woman I should marry surprisingly and miraculously ended in the medical school library. I was purposefully searching through the library for a misplaced magazine in which I could read about an upcoming event in Houston, hoping I could convince someone to go on a date with me. Unknowingly, I was on a God-ordained mission, unaware of how successfully my mission would soon be accomplished.

Shockingly, suddenly, and unexpectedly, my search for a godly wife came to an end. I believe I was divinely led to the audio/visual department, a rather strange place to look for a magazine. The woman working at the counter had a kind smile, a sparkle in her eye, and an aura about her which made it clear she was a child of the King. I could sense the glory of the Lord in Linda, and I liked it! God made us both immediately aware something amazing had happened. It was the most joyful moment in my then twenty-five years of life.

Just as happened in my decision to declare Jesus as Lord, God had ordained something of profound significance to happen in the briefest of moments. In the natural realm our meeting seemed random and unplanned, but I am confident the Holy Spirit choreographed the entire event. It was God's unpredictable but perfect plan, enacted at exactly the right moment, that supernaturally brought the two of us together to become one.

Seeking God's Kingdom First ✳

God knew the desires of my heart because He was the One who had placed them there long ago. The desires had become more important to me than the One who created them in me. He wisely would not allow them to be satisfied while I participated in the idolatry of seeking a wife on my own. The Spirit of wisdom (Isaiah 11:2) in Jesus is evident in the simple words of His powerful command and promise found in Matthew 6: "But seek first his kingdom and his righteousness, and all these things will be given to you as well" (v. 33).

The specific details and timing of your life story are quite different from mine. For all of us, though, lordship is the prerequisite for us to experience the full grandeur of God's plan. Many of us foolishly spend our lifetimes striving for the things we desire and need. The desires are good and the needs are real. However, the Father knows what we need before we ask Him (Matthew 6:8), and He is able and willing to "give good gifts to those who ask" (Matthew 7:11). God's Kingdom and righteousness must be the first priority if life is to be satisfying and abundant. When Jesus is Lord, His divine power will provide everything you and your marriage need for life and godliness (2 Peter 1:3). I believe "all these things" from Matthew 6:33 is inclusive of everything that is needed and more. A supernatural marriage flows in abundant blessings that are far beyond what we ask or imagine. God provides generously for His people, but only when they truly seek Him first. His lordship must be complete in our lives if we are to walk in the greatness of God's plan for supernatural marriage.

Chapter Seven

COMPLETE LORDSHIP:
LETTING GOD REIGN IN SPIRIT, SOUL, AND BODY

*G*od is passionate about you! Theologian Henri Nouwen said, "God [is] a jealous lover who wants every part of me all the time."[5] He has placed a capacity for passion within you and wants it used for its intended purposes, the greatest of which is to be passionate about Him. God's passion for you and your returning that passion back to Him is another way of describing the complete lordship I chose on that pivotal day in my last year of medical school.

Being passionate about God requires submitting all of who we are to Him. God wants complete lordship of our spirit, soul, and body. That sounds good in theory, but let's gets more practical. What does it look like in the perceivable world? How does it play out during earthly life? And, how in this world are we to get there?

---

[5]Henri Nouwen, *The Return of the Prodigal Son,* (New York: An Image Book, 1994), 17.

I want to show you, on a practical level, how to make Jesus Lord of your spirit, your soul, and even of your body. One way of looking at complete lordship can be found in the words of John the Baptist. In response to whether or not he was the Christ, John affirmed he was not and said, "I baptize you with water for repentance. But after me will come one who is more powerful than I, whose sandals I am not fit to carry. He will baptize you with the Holy Spirit and with fire" (Matthew 3:11).

BAPTISM OF WATER – LORDSHIP OF THE SPIRIT

"I baptize you with water for repentance."
Water = Lordship of the spirit

We all worship someone or something. The question is: Who or what do we worship? Do we worship the king of darkness or the King of Light? All mankind submits to one of two "lords." The question can be restated as this: Who is your Lord, Satan or Jesus? We cannot be partially saved; we are either saved or we are not saved. When we are saved, salvation is always complete because Jesus "is able to save completely those who come to God through him, because he always lives to intercede for them" (Hebrews 7:25). Our spirit is totally in the control and under the dominion of either God or Satan. There is no in-between. You cannot serve both God and the enemy; you cannot eat from the table of God and the table of demons (1 Corinthians 10:21).

Submitting to God in water baptism demonstrates our decision to acknowledge Jesus as Lord of our spirit. The concept of salvation is taught widely in the church because it is logical and understandable to the natural mind. I was blessed with salvation through Jesus at the age of eleven and was baptized in the swimming pool at a summer camp in Missouri. I was confused as to what God expected of me after that event, but my salvation was very real. At the time of salvation Jesus is concerned with the decisions of our hearts much more than the completeness of our human understanding.

Jesus' primary directive concerning the decisions of our heart is that to be saved we must believe He is the Son of God. In John 8:24, He declares, "If you do not believe that I am the one I claim to be, you will indeed die in your sins." Believing Jesus is the Son of God is not a one-time event, but the initiation of a lifelong process.

Jesus said to the religious people of the day, "You do not believe because you are not my sheep. My sheep listen to my voice; I know them, and they follow me. I give them eternal life, and they shall never perish; no one can snatch them out of my hand" (John 10:26-28). The point of verse 26 is that sheep know who their shepherd is. They listen to his voice and follow his instruction. They have an ongoing relationship with the shepherd who protects them and supplies all they need. As we relate to Jesus as our trusted Shepherd, we act out our faith in Him. Jesus desires that we know Him, hear Him, and obediently follow Him wherever He leads us. The process of intimate relational connectedness between the Savior and the saved brings joy and satisfaction to both involved. No one can snatch us out of His hand. Nothing can separate us from Him or eternal life filled with His love. Paul pondered this question of what would separate us from God's love and then answered this most perplexing question:

Who shall separate us from the love of Christ? Shall trouble or hardship or persecution or famine or nakedness or danger or sword?

No, in all these things we are more than conquerors through him who loved us. For I am convinced that neither death nor life, neither angels nor demons, neither the present nor the future, nor any powers, neither height nor depth, nor anything else in all creation, will be able to separate us from the love of God that is in Christ Jesus our Lord.

– Romans 8:35, 37-39

Our Savior wants those who are saved to be completely immersed in a relationship with Him so that He can change them into who they were created to be. Salvation is not a stagnant state of being. It is the first stage in a dynamic process of becoming more like Jesus. True conversion produces a connection with the eternal source of transformation. Many have thought conversion to be the end, but really it is just the beginning of a life-long process of growing in godliness.

The desire of Jesus' heart is for us to be wrapped up in a relationship with Him. "How great is the love the Father has lavished on us, that we should be called children of God! And that is what we are!" (1 John 3:1). Through Jesus we are adopted as God's sons and receive the Holy Spirit as a deposit, guaranteeing our full inheritance while, as God's possession, we go through the process of becoming fully redeemed (Ephesians 1:3-14).

Water baptism involves the immersion of our physical body in water so that nothing is left untouched and nothing remains exposed. It declares to both the kingdom of this world and the Kingdom of our Lord, "Jesus is Lord of my spirit!" In salvation, our spirit is completely enveloped in the living water that flows from the throne of God. No area within our spirit is left untouched by His eternal glory, and no part of our spirit remains exposed to the powers of darkness. When Jesus is sincerely established as Lord of our spirit, our salvation is complete and secure.

BAPTISM OF FIRE – LORDSHIP OF THE SOUL

"He will baptize you ... with fire."
Fire = Lordship of the soul

Many Christians are as I was until two weeks before meeting Linda in the medical school library. They have honestly accepted Jesus as Lord of their spirits, which is synonymous with salvation, but have never made the decision to pursue complete lordship of their souls. The soul is composed of the mind, will, emotions, and imagination. These aspects of who we are can be perceived and understood reasonably well in the natural realm. They are gifts from God that help us understand the attributes of God, as He made us in His own image (Genesis 1:26). If our desire is to truly honor God, He requires lordship to be evident in all four areas of our soul.[6]

To properly position ourselves in relation to God, we must make a conscious choice to make Him Lord of every part of who we are. Although a man makes this decision in the natural realm, God directs its implementation and destiny through the supernatural realm. At salvation the fiery presence of God invades and inhabits the spirit of a man. The ultimate plan is that this fire would spread to invade and eternally change every aspect of the soul – mind, will, emotions, and the imagination.

The Mind

Romans 8:6-7 says, "The mind of a sinful man is death, but the mind controlled by the Spirit is life and peace; the sinful mind is hostile to God. It does not submit to God's law, nor can it do

---

[6]For the purposes of this discussion, "mind" will be used in a limited way to include the intellectual functions of reasoning and comprehension.

so." The mind controlled by the Holy Spirit is willing and able to submit fully to Jesus' lordship – it is "life and peace." We are told in Romans 12:2, "Do not conform any longer to the pattern of this world, but be transformed by the renewing of your mind." This transformation is supernaturally accomplished in our minds through the supernatural touch of God. It cannot be achieved within the natural realm. Mind renewal requires divine revelation.

Our way of thinking can be so incredibly changed that Paul confidently proclaims, "We have the mind of Christ" (1 Corinthians 2:16). But, for this to happen we must relinquish control of our human minds. If we can only accept patterns of thinking that are consistent with what we learned in the world system, we set ourselves up "against the knowledge of God." But we are to demolish the arguments and pretensions that rise up against God: "We demolish arguments and every pretension that sets itself up against the knowledge of God, and we take captive every thought to make it obedient to Christ" (2 Corinthians 10:5). Obedience to Christ demands that every thought be deferential to His complete control. By the power of the Holy Spirit, we must learn to captivate our thoughts in order to bring them into complete obedience to Christ. Jesus must become Lord of our mind if complete lordship is to take place in the realm of the soul.

The Will

As our wills are transformed by the Spirit of God within us, they too become more and more like Jesus, who declared, "I have come down from heaven not to do my will but to do the will of him who sent me" (John 6:38). When we allow Jesus to be Lord of our lives, the desire of our hearts becomes just like that of Jesus when, submitting to Father, He prayed, "Your kingdom come, your will be done on earth as it is in heaven" (Matthew 6:10). As this submission to authority is individually personalized, it becomes "not my will, but yours be done" (Luke 22:42). We are children of God and our heartfelt desire is that our wills be controlled by, and consistent with, the will of our Father. With yielding to God's will as the default setting of our lives, obedience rarely becomes an issue. Jesus must become Lord of our wills if we are to walk in His complete lordship.

The Emotions

When Jesus is Lord of our emotions we are freed and empowered to use them in the ways that best honor Him. Instead of being only reactions to the triumphs and disappointments of life, our emotions become useful tools which God can use to accomplish His purposes through us as we relate to Him and others on earth. The Holy Spirit must lead us in the use of our emotions just as we allow God to lead us in our thoughts, words, and actions.

Because of the absence of visible emotions in some churches, believers often joke about their fellowships as being "the frozen chosen." God wants us to reverently honor Him, while at the same time He desires a warm and intimate relationship with us, His dearly loved children (Ephesians 5:1). We have received the Spirit of sonship by which we can emotionally cry "Abba" to our loving Father (Romans 8:15; Galatians 4:6). I am confident it pleases God when He sees tears of emotion in our eyes as we express to Him our heartfelt love.

It is impossible to develop a true love relationship with God without becoming emotionally involved. It is unimaginable that a bride could honestly express her love to her groom on their wedding day with no emotion in her voice. Can passionate love be expressed without emotion? I believe it cannot. As we grow in intimacy with the Father, He and we become emotionally involved with each other. His emotions become ours in each situation we encounter. We delight in circumstances that bring Him joy and we grieve with God in situations that cause Him sorrow. Emotions fully in submission to God are incredibly useful in building the Kingdom around the One who is love.

The Imagination

The imagination is the creative component placed within each of us by our astoundingly creative Maker. The destiny of this gift is that we would participate with God in using it for the strengthening of the Kingdom and for the completion of His plan. God consistently exhibits inconceivable inventiveness in both the natural and supernatural realms. We can connect with God's imaginative nature through prophetic acts, creative writing, story telling, creative evangelism, visions, and even music. God frequently speaks to my imagination by means of dreams in the night. Through dreams we can receive clear understanding of the past and present as well as prophetic revelation of the future.

I was in a situation last year in which it would soon be necessary to make a decision as to which way to go in my life. Both ways seemed logical and good to my natural mind. But it became increasingly difficult to continue putting off the decision. One night, as Linda and I prayed together just before going to sleep, we asked God to give me a dream in the night that would clearly answer my question. I had a very vivid dream that night about driving a car at highway speed. The inside of the windshield rapidly developed a thick sheet of ice, completely obscuring my view. Unable to see the highway, I slowed and stopped as quickly as possible. Opening the door, I saw the car had stopped just in time to avoid crossing a four lane intersection full of traffic. I then noticed the smell of exhaust fumes. I was barely able to escape from the car before being overcome by the carbon monoxide. It was clear that I was safe, but only because I had quickly exited the situation.

Because God answered our prayers that night by giving me a dream, I was able to make the decision I needed. Through the dream God clearly told me it was unwise for me to continue in the activity I was questioning. It was obvious to me what decision should be made because the dream was so clear and vivid. God spoke to me through my imagination to answer our urgent question.

Lordship of our imaginations can be proclaimed each night in prayer as sleep and dreams are approached. Often at bedtime, Linda and I declare Jesus as our Lord and ask Him to sanctify our dreams. God is demonstrated to be Lord of our imaginations when we request God to speak to us in dreams, as we ask the Holy Spirit for interpretation of dreams, and when we are faithful to the vision and instruction God reveals to us through them. Just as is repeatedly demonstrated in the Bible, dreams are an amazing and powerful means of communication between the created and Creator. If we are to fulfill the purposes for which we were created, God must be fully in control of our imaginations.

God's Fire Refines All Four Parts of Our Soul

When John the Baptist said that Jesus would "baptize you ... with fire," he predicted the means by which God would achieve true lordship of all four parts of the soul in those who desire transformation. The acceptance of lordship leads to radical changes within us that can only be accomplished through the holy fire of God. His cleansing fire is incredibly valuable to anyone willing to submit to it. Those who yield to God welcome this fire and are blessed through its refining power. Those in rebellion against God fear His fire, for they know the intensity of its holiness could destroy them.

It is a dreadful thing to fall into the hands of the living God. - Hebrews 10:31

Fire goes before him and consumes his foes on every side. His lightning lights up the world; the earth sees and trembles. The mountains melt like wax before the Lord, before the Lord of all the earth. - Psalm 97:3-5

For our "God is a consuming fire." - Hebrews 12:29

Eight times in the Bible, God is referred to as "a consuming fire" (Hebrews 12:29). In time we will all be fully exposed to the consuming fire of God. As believers we do not run to escape God's holy fire because we know it is completely good. Within the fire of God is profound blessing. If asked, God will continually baptize us with His fire. It will refine us like silver and test us like gold. When refined by His fire we can call on His name and He will answer us. He will say, "They are my people" and we will say, "The Lord is our God" (Zechariah 13:9). We grow in intimacy with God as His fire refines us. This process of refining makes us more pure and we become more holy like the One whose flames transform us. While at first we may be afraid of the fire of God, with time we learn to welcome it.

Those who have not allowed Jesus to be Lord of their souls remain afraid of God's consuming fire. They are full of dread when they hear this concept or read through some of these Scriptures. His fire is coming and they know they are not prepared for it. Due to lack of obedience they are not allowed to deeply experience the satisfying nature of God's holy love. His perfect love is the only way to drive out this fear of His fire (1 John 4:18). When Jesus is Lord of the soul, this perfect love is received as a glorious gift from God. There is no longer a place within us or outside of us from which fear can destroy the peace received from Christ. When God's holy love has penetrated deeply into our hearts, and when we truly know[7] Him, our response to the consuming fire of God is eternally shifted from complete dread to pure delight because one of our greatest desires is to be like our Father in heaven.

THE BAPTISM OF THE HOLY SPIRIT— LORDSHIP OF THE BODY

"He will baptize you with the Holy Spirit." Holy Spirit = Lordship of the body

By the time Linda and I met, we were both serious about pursuing complete lordship. Certainly there remained large stockpiles of wood, hay, and stubble which could only be removed by the refining fire of God, but we were willing to submit to that fire (1 Corinthians 3:10-15). At times the fire seemed very hot, even painful as it burned away impurities such as selfishness and pride. With time it became more and more evident that God's refining was useful, valuable, and completely good. Eventually we learned to welcome the fire, asking God to burn away everything that remained in us that was not from Him. The process is never complete in this life. In fact, the process of sanctification will continue until the day we die. We continue today asking for more of the refining fire of God to purify our hearts so we can greater reflect the glory of God in this world.

Through the years our ability to consistently obey God im-

---

[7]The Greek word used here is *ginosko* – which is a rich and intimate knowing of God similar to how a husband and wife know each other intimately (Matthew 1:25).

proved dramatically. Honoring God through obedience truly became the desire of our hearts. Yet, we both began to sense there was something available to us as believers that was beyond what we understood or had previously experienced. We had been baptized in water, proclaiming Jesus as Lord of our spirits. And we willingly submitted to baptism in God's refining fire, accepting Him to be Lord of our souls. However, though it had been our desire for years, we did not know how to receive the baptism of the Holy Spirit.

For us, this third baptism was neither understandable nor achievable until we passed through the events described earlier.[8] Receiving the baptism of the Holy Spirit demanded that we surrender control of our very flesh into the hands of God. It required that we accept Him as Lord of our bodies, allowing things to happen to us and through us which made no sense to our human minds. The interaction of God's Spirit with our human flesh resulted in manifestations which were considered socially unacceptable by many, but eternally valuable. When we experienced these things of the Spirit we found them to be life changing, repeatable, and astonishingly real.

More important than supernaturally encountering God, though, is being supernaturally transformed by Him. These experiences with the Holy Spirit are intended to equip, empower, and embolden us to bear much fruit. When the Spirit is active within us we receive an increased knowledge of who God is and a better understanding of His glorious plan for us. The goodness of God draws us into a love relationship filled with love, peace, joy, and a strong desire to honor Him through obedience to His will.

---

[8]See Chapter 4, entitled, "Texas Ablaze: Our Journey into Supernatural Encounters with God," for more information on the events we went through to get us to the place to receive the Holy Spirit in such a valuable way.

The progression of lordship from spirit to soul to body is not unique to our experience. Although commitment to God can proceed in any order, this is a common pattern of spiritual formation. It is important to remember, however, that God is sovereign and interacts with His children individually in ways that are solely of His choosing. Every person has different stories to tell as to what they have experienced upon encountering the Spirit of God. To each the Holy Spirit seems as unpredictable as the wind. In John 3:8 Jesus reminds us, "The wind blows wherever it pleases. You hear its sound, but you cannot tell where it comes from or where it is going. So it is with everyone born of the Spirit." Regardless of how each of us may experience and recognize the baptism of the Holy Spirit in our soul and physical body, it is vitally important that our intimate connectedness with the Spirit continue. God touches us with His Spirit to initiate a lifelong spiritual communion intended to lead us into lives which powerfully demonstrate His divine presence and eternal glory within us.

God places within each of us an intense desire and an insatiable hunger for more of Him. At salvation we taste and see that the Lord is incredibly good, whetting our spiritual appetite for more of Him. Our spirit is filled with God, who is the "spring of living water" (Jeremiah 2:13). For the first time in our lives we begin to experience true peace that transcends our understanding (Philippians 4:7) and we know in our hearts that we will never thirst again (John 4:14). As we ask and receive more of the Holy Spirit (Luke 11:13), there is an overflowing of God's presence from our spirits into the realm of the soul. Filled with the Spirit of Holy God, we "hunger and thirst for righteousness" (Matthew 5:6). As God transforms us by the renewing of our minds (Romans 12:2), our will becomes the same as His. The Holy Spirit invades our souls like a refining fire and makes them fully subject to the lordship of

God. But, our insatiable hunger and unquenchable thirst for God does not stop when He is Lord only of our spirit and soul. He must become Lord of all!

Lord of All

Seven times in the New International Version Bible God is referred to as "Lord of all."[9] Seven is the number of completeness. Honoring Him requires that His lordship be complete. Jesus is pleased when we accept Him as Lord of our spirits and honored when He is, in fact, Lord of our souls. However, neither He nor we will be satisfied until He is Lord of our bodies as well. Our innate desire for God prompts us to continue asking, seeking, and knocking (Matthew 7:7) as we passionately invite Him to fully enter every part of who we are.

Our loving Father in heaven is eager to "give the Holy Spirit to those who ask him" (Luke 11:13). When the Holy Spirit is poured into a man's heart "streams of living water will flow from within him" (John 7:38). The river of God's Spirit completely overwhelms the capacity of our spirits and floods through our souls. When our minds and wills cease to resist the flow of the Spirit (Acts 7:51), it can suddenly invade the realm of our bodies. Our flesh is useful in demonstrating the glory of the Lord, but can in no way contain it. As the supernatural stream of the Holy Spirit passes into and through our natural bodies it is not surprising that our flesh would respond in extraordinary and unexpected ways.

Bodily responses such as tears, laughter, shaking, and losing the ability to stand are manifestations in the natural realm of supernatural events. Physical changes occur within us when our flesh is invaded by the glorious presence of God. What we refer to as

---

[9] See Joshua 3:11, 13; Psalm 97:5; Micah 4:13; Zechariah 4:14; Acts 10:36; Romans 10:12.

"the laws of nature" no longer apply when control of our flesh is in submission to the superior nature of *El Elyon*, the God Most High.

God's Kingdom Manifested Through You

The early disciples were confident that, through them, God would heal all kinds of diseases. In fact, they even prayed: "Stretch out your hand to heal and perform miraculous signs and wonders through the name of your holy servant Jesus." Then Luke comments further: "After they prayed, the place where they were meeting was shaken. And they were all filled with the Holy Spirit and spoke the word of God boldly" (Acts 4:30-31). They had witnessed Jesus' healing the sick and raising the dead. They had been filled with the same Holy Spirit that empowered Jesus to demonstrate the power and glory of God on earth. Stephen, Paul, Barnabus, and the seventy-two sent out by Jesus were also among those who carried within themselves the actual presence of the living God and transformed the natural realm surrounding them with the authority they had received. The initial command was given in Matthew 10:8 to the twelve disciples to preach the Kingdom of God and to "heal the sick, raise the dead, cleanse those who have leprosy, [and] drive out demons." This command was later given to the seventy-two (Luke 10:1-12) and later told to be passed on to all the disciples (Mark 16:15-20).

We and our marriages can be filled with the same Holy Spirit as Jesus was. We have the same ability to "heal and perform miraculous signs and wonders" as believers sent directly by Jesus in the Gospels and later throughout the book of Acts.

God uses miraculous signs and wonders to demonstrate His supernatural power and eternal glory in such a way that they can be perceived in the natural realm. It is God's desire that you personally experience these things. Encountering Him with all of your senses allows you to know Him in ways unavailable through the mind alone. Watching others participate in healings, signs, and wonders can prepare you to allow the Holy Spirit to manifest as you finally submit to His control. Before you know it, God may be using your hands to lay on the sick, your tongue to prophesy words of destiny and hope, and His authority in you to cast out demons!

When the Pharisees asked Jesus when the Kingdom of God would come, He replied saying, "The kingdom of God does not come with your careful observation, nor will people say, 'Here it is,' or 'There it is,' because the kingdom of God is within you" (Luke 17:20-21). The Kingdom not becoming visible by careful observation was applicable to the Pharisees and is equally valid for each of us today. We cannot receive Kingdom power and authority by only watching others manifest His glory. We must allow ourselves to be fully available to Him.

We are baptized with the Holy Spirit when we, as the bride of Christ, consent to become one flesh with Jesus, our Bridegroom. Holy Spirit baptism is a demonstration of our intimate and uninhibited love relationship with Him. It is the perceivable entry of the supernatural realm of God into the natural realm of our human body. In this encounter we allow the glory of the Spirit of Jesus unlimited access to every aspect of who we are. There is nothing available in earthly life that more profoundly alters our ability to know God, our understanding of who we are, and our capacity to fulfill our destiny.

Free Access Through the Holy Spirit

The baptism of the Holy Spirit initiates the flow of the river of God's glory within us. The tangible flow of this living water has a beginning but no intended end. God's glory is continuously available to those He inhabits. As David implied in Psalm 139, God is present in the heavens, in the depths, and everywhere in between. David reflected, "Where can I go from your Spirit? Where can I flee from your presence? If I go up to the heavens, you are there; if I make my bed in the depths, you are there" (Psalm 139:7-8). In theological language He is omnipresent. God "is not far from each one of us" (Acts 17:27) and He is in us (Job 32:8; Ezekiel 36:26-27), on us (Acts 2:3), and around us (Psalm 3:3). He will never leave you or forsake you (Deuteronomy 31:6). God is readily accessible to those who desire an intimate relationship with Him.

One of my favorite teachings that I've heard was from Todd Bentley, several years ago, when He spoke about "stepping in and stepping out" of God's glory. God is always present regardless of our location or our circumstances. With desire and practice we can learn to "step in" to God's presence, consciously experiencing His supernatural presence. Interruptions or distractions of life, such as a ringing telephone, can disappoint us by shifting our awareness completely back into the natural realm. But, just as easily as we stepped out of perceiving the glory of God, we can quickly step back in again. Since learning this, Linda and I have been thrilled to have the ability to simply and beautifully experience the Holy Spirit's presence at will, not only as individuals but also as one flesh in our marriage.

We heard a parallel teaching by Patricia King during her Glory School. She taught us that any vision, dream, or heavenly encounter given by God becomes the possession of the recipient. These supernatural experiences can be reactivated in the future by those who own them. They are given to us by God to reveal His mysteries to us and to bless us. I totally agree with her! These glorious encounters with heaven are eternally alive within us. They can be repeatedly relived to remind us of God's glorious presence and our position as His dearly loved children.

My point is that God gives us the desire and the ability to be intimately connected with Him in an ongoing, eternal relationship. Yes, at times we must patiently wait for Him and continually pray for His glory to come. But God is honored when we passionately pursue Him and He is pleased to share His amazing love, His beautiful glory, and His unfathomable mysteries by pouring His Spirit into us when we seek Him first.

Too often we are dependent on others to teach us how to have a deep relationship with God. Teachers and mentors are wonderful and needed by all of us. But God cannot be truly known through words and instruction alone. No one in marriage becomes a great lover without experiencing their spouse in every conceivable way. It is no different in our relationship with God. We will never learn to intimately relate to the Lover of our souls through the teaching of those who know Him. True knowledge and understanding of our supernatural God can only be obtained directly from the source, not just hearing about the source. God is the source of everything we need. Peter said it is "His divine power [that] has given us everything we need for life and godliness through our knowledge of him who called us by his own glory and goodness" (2 Peter 1:3). Through the divine power of the Holy Spirit we have been given free access to the spiritual realm.

> However, as it is written: "No eye has seen, no ear has heard, no mind has conceived what God has prepared for those who love him" – but God has revealed it to us by his Spirit.

> The Spirit searches all things, even the deep things of God. For who among men knows the thoughts of a man except the man's spirit within him? In the same way no one knows the thoughts of God except the Spirit of God. We have not received the spirit of the world but the Spirit who is from God, that we may understand what God has freely given us. This

is what we speak, not in words taught us by human wisdom but in words taught by the Spirit, expressing spiritual truths in spiritual words. The man without the Spirit does not accept the things that come from the Spirit of God, for they are foolishness to him, and he cannot understand them, because they are spiritually discerned.   – 1 Corinthians 2:9-14

The baptism of the Holy Spirit is the least understood and the most controversial subject in the twenty-first century church. The teachings of Jesus and the concepts of godly living explained in the Bible can be understood to a degree by the mind of anyone who is desiring to learn them. It is impossible, however, to communicate with words or even comprehend with human intellect the things of the Spirit. As Paul says, "they are spiritually discerned" (2:14). "God is spirit, and his worshipers must worship in spirit and in truth" (John 4:24). The deep and intimate things He longs to reveal to us as His loved children can only be received as we commune with Him spirit to Spirit. The richest and most intimate revelations from God must first be experienced in the flesh before they can be even partially understood by the mind. For us to "accept the things that come from the Spirit of God" requires that we concede to God's lordship of our bodies.

LORD OF SPIRIT, SOUL, AND BODY

Lordship is the key to establishing and maintaining an intimate love relationship with God. He will not allow us to fully share in His love, His glory, His power, or the fulfillment of His plan if we compromise in any of these three areas. We must not settle for incomplete lordship. God's desire is that we be transformed to become holy just as He is holy (1 Peter 1:16). This transformation will be delayed, stopped, or even reversed if we stubbornly refuse to relinquish control of any part of our lives.

The wonderful thing is that if we seek God we "will find him if [we] look for him with all [our] heart and with all [our] soul" (Deuteronomy 4:29; Jeremiah 29:13). When we truly seek Him first He naturally becomes Lord of every aspect of who we are and provides literally everything we need. God becomes our closest Friend and most trusted Lover. He also knows our need for relational intimacy with others and is quite willing to provide exactly what we need.

Intimacy with God makes it possible for us to successfully enter the extreme and satisfying intimacy of marriage. When His supernatural love is received in our spirits, honored in our souls, and consummated in our bodies, we are enabled to function beyond the limits of natural human relationships. With the Holy Spirit resting upon us we become able to operate within supernatural marriage, filled with the spiritual essence of wisdom, understanding, counsel, power, knowledge, and fear of the Lord (Isaiah 11:2). Through complete lordship and intimacy with God, marriage becomes fully what God intended it to be in the Garden of Eden, where, for a time, God's will was done on earth exactly as it was in heaven.

Paul prayed for the Thessalonians and also for us:

May God himself, the God of peace, sanctify you through and through. May your whole spirit, soul and body be kept blameless at the coming of our Lord Jesus Christ.

– 1 Thessalonians 5:23

This "blameless" state is accomplished when God Himself sanctifies us, which is making us holy "through and through." Only God can make us holy as individuals and it is only God who can bring two believers together as one to establish true holy matrimony. There is no greater joy in life than experiencing "the God of peace" in the center of a supernatural marriage. Intimate and fulfilling oneness between man, woman and God can only be experienced when Jesus is established as Lord of our entire being – spirit, soul, and body. He must be "Lord of all" (Acts 10:36).

Part Two

GOD'S PLAN

FOR

SUPERNATURAL MARRIAGE

A WARNING FROM ZECHARIAH FOUR

DESPISING SMALL THINGS

The following chapters discuss types of marriages which differ in their relational compatibility, consistency with biblical values, and connectedness with the Holy Spirit. Reading this could be discouraging to some who feel that their marital relationship is so far from supernatural that improvement is impossible. Please allow me to remind you that nothing is impossible for our limitless God (Matthew 19:26). God Himself placed the desire for supernatural marriage within you long ago and progress has already begun. It is not a coincidence you are reading this book. The Holy Spirit Himself has led you to it!

Your attraction to learning more about supernatural marriage may seem to be a small thing but is actually quite *huge!* After conquering Babylon in 539 B.C., King Cyrus of Persia appointed Zerubbabel to lead a remnant of Israel as they returned to their homeland. After a period of years Zerubbabel was becoming discouraged by the immense challenges of rebuilding the temple in

Jerusalem. God sent the prophet Zechariah to encourage him by telling him that not only had he started rebuilding the temple, but he would finish the project as well. Zechariah said to Zerubbabel, "The hands of Zerubbabel have laid the foundation of this temple; his hands will also complete it. Then you will know that the Lord Almighty has sent me to you. Who despises the day of small things?" (Zechariah 4:9-10). The governor of Judea was advised by God to not despise "small things." We must realize that everything God does in us or through us is of great and eternal significance. Nothing done by God is ever small.

As you read the next chapters, it is helpful to recognize where you and your marriage presently are. Recognition of present reality is usually a good thing. Be honest with yourself as to the current state of your marriage, but be encouraged to know that progress has already begun. God has placed a desire in you for change and transformation – a desire in you for supernatural marriage. You can trust God to "carry it on to completion" (Philippians 1:6). As you proceed, it is critically important that you aim for the absolute best in your relationships, both with God and your spouse in marriage. You must "press on toward the goal to win the prize" (Philippians 3:14).

In marriage, always aim for the highest and the best. Do not compromise God's perfect plan for you by settling for a partially holy matrimony – fulfilling only part of what God's plans and purposes are for your marriage. Regardless of the current state of your marital relationship, you are an integral part of the bride of Christ. You are being adorned, perfected, and prepared to become exactly who God created you to be. His plan for your marriage is that both you and your spouse, as one, become intimately involved with the Bridegroom Himself. May God's will be done in your life on earth just as it is in heaven (Matthew 6:10). Amazing things can happen in His supernatural realm!

Chapter Eight

THE PLAN OF MARRIAGE

ATTACK ON THE PLAN OF MARRIAGE

"For I know the plans I have for you," declares the Lord, "plans to prosper you and not to harm you, plans to give you hope and a future." —Jeremiah 29:11

*L*inda and I have often quoted this passage from Jeremiah to our two boys in an effort to encourage them or push them on a little further toward who God intended them to become. It is a basic axiom in our understanding of God's perfect plan for us as individuals and in our marriage. In all honesty His plans have been "immeasurably more than all we ask or imagine" (Ephesians 3:20). God has shocked both Linda and me with the depth of love and the closeness of relational intimacy we have been allowed to experience. He is "the God of hope" who fills us with joy and peace, that we "may overflow with hope by the power of the Holy Spirit" (Romans 15:13). God is willing and able to prosper us in such a way as to fulfill the hope He has placed in us concerning the future. The manifestation of His divine plan often exceeds our human understanding of what we should hope for.

Even in the secular world most couples enter marriage optimistically, with great expectations for the future. On our wedding day Linda and I really had no clue what we were getting into, but we dreamed of a future with optimism and excitement! The hope for marriage to be filled with love and satisfaction is placed in us by God as an achievable goal. It is His passionate desire that each marriage be established upon and built around His glorious and holy presence. God's goals for marriage are so high He even uses the covenant of marriage as a prototype of the intense love relationship that is to exist between Christ and the church, which culminates in His being united as one flesh with her when He returns as the Bridegroom (Ephesians 5:22-33). God is more than able to fulfill His plans for our marriages. With God's supernatural presence and love within us, we have a specific promise that our hope will not disappoint us (Romans 5:5).

There is no part of human life that Satan attacks more frequently and violently than the covenant of marriage. He assaults its gloriously planned potential through discord, division, selfishness, pride, lust, anger, rage, and every other imaginable sin. Why does this happen? It is simply because Satan is terrified of God-centered marriage. He most aggressively assaults the most dangerous enemy of his evil empire. Each of these methods of attack is a means of shifting the focus of marriage out of the eternal Kingdom of our Lord and into the temporary kingdom of this world.

Supernatural marriage is a fortress that houses a divinely forged alloy of tremendous strength and inestimable eternal value. In it man, woman, and God are brought together as one flesh to create an entity for which Satan has no reliable way to attack, no useful battle plan to defeat, and no effective weapon to destroy. This type of marriage is a powerful and effective structure designed by the wisest Architect and constructed by the most masterful Builder. Neither Satan nor any other power in the kingdom of darkness can prevent the completion of this plan.

Marriage was established prior to the introduction of sin into the world. Satan attacked the first marriage through deception and confusion before the relationship between Adam, Eve, and God had time to become mature. The open door for this attack was disobedience, which was based on a lack of submission to God's lordship over the lives of our first parents. Our primary desire must remain being obedient to God as we run the race to fulfill every hope He has placed within us. God is 100% faithful (1 Corinthians 10:13) and we emulate Him by being completely faithful, both in action and in thought, to our marriage partner. But we must never think we have reached a height from which it is impossible to fall (Revelation 2:5).

The first marriage was badly damaged by Satan before its blessings could be extended to the next generation. Each supernatural marriage multiplies its blessing by passing them on to "a thousand generations" (Deuteronomy 5:10). If Adam and Eve had not sinned at that point in time, Satan's plan to "steal and kill and destroy" (John 10:10) could have been effectively neutralized for years to come. Instead, their children were punished "for the sin of the fathers to the third and fourth generation" (Numbers 14:18).

God's plan for marriage has always been wise and absolutely good. Adam and Eve were joined by God to be husband and wife in the first supernatural marriage. Together they shared abundant life in the most idyllic of settings, but their rebellion against God started a death spiral that nearly drew all of mankind into the abyss. Their son Cain was filled with murderous jealousy against his brother Abel (Genesis 4:1-16). Only nine generations after Adam, man's wickedness had become so great that God chose to destroy all but Noah's family with a great flood. The biblical narrative records it like this: "The Lord saw how great man's wickedness on the earth had become, and that every inclination of the thoughts of his heart was only evil all the time" (Genesis 6:5). The horrific destruction brought to the world was initiated when Satan successfully separated Adam, Eve, and their supernatural marriage from intimate connectedness with God.

HOPE IN THE WEDDING FEAST OF THE LAMB

We no longer live in the Adamic era. We have received the law and have seen God's passionate desire to bless His people, the physical and spiritual children of Abraham. His perfect plan has been prophesied, revealed, and enacted with power and glory. Throughout the ages, His prophetic word has been written and spoken, showing us more and more of who He is, why we were created, and what we are asked to do. God demonstrated His perfect love to us through the life, crucifixion, and resurrection of His Son. Jesus physically left the earth as He ascended into heaven, but spiritually blessed us as believers with continual access to the Father and Himself through the precious gift of the Holy Spirit (Luke 24:49).

The children of Adam *knew of* God, but did not *know* God in the same way their parents had known Him. Their children didn't know what it was like to walk with God without the presence of sin in their lives. They didn't understand, nor could they comprehend, what it was like for God to come and walk with them "in the cool of the day" (Genesis 3:8). This glorious union between Adam, Eve, and God was disrupted through the fall. The generations that followed never knew the intimate communion with God which

Adam and Eve had experienced prior to the fall, because their close connectedness with the source of all holiness had been lost. They lost their love relationship with Him and abandoned their desire for truth. Adam's descendants traded radiant light for the blackest darkness and eventually lost their very lives in the flood of God's vengeance.

But we live eternally "as children of [the] light" (Ephesians 5:8). We have possession of the Truth and He has set us free (John 8:32). God has placed His Holy Spirit within us that we will be strengthened by constant connection to Him and His glory. We know Him because He is actually in us - spirit, soul, and body.

God has established an intense love relationship between Himself and us which is so full of life, peace, joy, and love, that we best understand it through His analogy of the last and perfect marriage which John describes in Revelation: "Let us rejoice and be glad and give him glory! For the wedding of the Lamb has come, and his bride has made herself ready" (Revelation 19:7).

During an interlude in Robert Stearns' version of the song, "Dance with Me" (recorded on the worship CD *The River 5: Dance With Me*), prophetic minister Mickey Robinson makes a spontaneous declaration describing the flawlessly choreographed relationship God is establishing between Jesus and the church as they prepare to dance together at the ultimate wedding feast.

Behold, I tell you a mystery: the Lord does want to dance. We are in a season that is called "the season of the bride and the Bridegroom." God will reveal the mystery of the bride and the Bridegroom. And yet I tell you now, the important part of this is that you be moved by He, the Bridegroom; not of your own accord, not of your own initiative, not of a certain body of teaching, not of a certain popularity, not of a certain gift. For in the true dance of romance the Bridegroom leads and the bride devotionally, beautifully and harmoniously follows.

The bride must make herself ready before the Bridegroom will return. Each believer is part of the church, which is being transformed into the glorious bride of Christ. The Spirit of Christ within us literally changes who we are. With His perfect love flowing through us, we are enabled to passionately love the Bridegroom with consistency and selflessness. Christ's call to intimacy becomes the intense desire of our hearts as our hearts are touched and transformed by God's great love. We learn with time that wherever He leads us in the dance is always exactly where it is best for us to go. The romance is real and safe; it is completely fulfilling because of the holiness and faithfulness of the One who masterfully leads us through the dance of life.

Our love relationship with the flawless Bridegroom leads us into an unstoppable hope for the future. With Christ in us we cannot be defeated. He is so faithful that nothing can separate us from Him. Filled with the love of the Father and empowered with the anointing of the Holy Spirit, there is no limit to what can be accomplished in the dance with Jesus, our Bridegroom. Together with Him "we rejoice in the hope of the glory of God" (Romans 5:2).

With confidence and boldness we declare the truth of the coming wedding of the holy Bridegroom and the perfected bride. Paul says, "since we have such a hope, we are very bold" (2 Corinthians 3:12). So without question, the bride and the Bridegroom will gloriously become one.

We who "have such a hope" must extend it to include hope of reaching the glorious potential God has established for holy matrimony between believers. With God's Spirit in us, our own marriages can be viewed with this same unstoppable and indefeatable hope. With His glorious presence in the center of our marriages there is no limit to the degree of supernatural transformation that can occur.

Although we are aware of imperfections in our own marriages and in the marriages of others, we are not to be discouraged by them. The hope that we see in the wedding feast of the Lamb described in Revelation 19 is something to be anticipated, but we must "wait for it patiently" (Romans 8:25). Regardless of where we are or where we have been, God is willing and able to increase our faith, raise our level of obedience, and draw us into our destiny as His dearly loved children (Ephesians 5:1). He is the God of the best, the finest, and the maximum. Everything about God is far beyond what we experience or expect within the natural realm. He is completely holy and absolutely faithful. His wisdom is boundless and His power exceeds our imaginations. God is completely capable of providing everything we need for life and godliness. No matter where we are currently in our relationship with God, He is always planning opportunities for us to advance further with Him in the supernatural realm.

There is a glorious future ordained for each of us before even one of our days comes to be (Psalm 139:16). As we wait patiently, our hope is very real. Paul says it like this: "But if we hope for what we do not yet have, we wait for it patiently" (Romans 8:25). God is quite capable of supernaturally leading us, as individuals and in our marital relationships, into the complete fulfillment of His plan and purpose for our lives.

CONSTANT TRANSFORMATION AND CONTINUAL INCREASE

Until perfection is reached there will always be an opportunity, even an expectation from God, for further advancement in our lives and improvement in our marriages. As we learn to live and love like Jesus, we are "transformed into his likeness with ever-increasing glory" (2 Corinthians 3:18). In fact, the Christian life is one of consistent transformation and continual increase in God's Kingdom. When our marriage unions reflect the glory of the Lord brightly, we truly honor the King of Glory. The only way His glory can shine out from our marriages is that it first be supernaturally received "from the Lord, who is the Spirit" (2 Corinthians 3:18). The latest relational techniques or modes of communication can obviously help, but it is ultimately spiritual connectedness with each other and with God that we need in our marriages.

God's Kingdom is one of continual increase. There is no limit to the extent to which He can demonstrate His glorious presence within our marital relationships. Isaiah prophesied about the continual increase of God's reign when he said, "Of the increase of his government and peace there will be no end. He will reign on David's throne and over his kingdom, establishing and upholding it with justice and righteousness from that time on and forever. The zeal of the Lord Almighty will accomplish this" (Isaiah 9:7).

God's plans for our marriages are perfectly good. As one flesh we are given the privilege of fully participating in the increasing glory of Jesus' Kingdom. But this increase does not come through moderate effort or part-time interest. Only "the zeal of the Lord Almighty" will accomplish this. Directly or indirectly, the Holy Spirit imparts this zeal into the participants of every supernatural marriage. If we do not carry "the zeal of the Lord," we cannot fully play our part in increasing the glory of God. He desires that we zealously participate in every aspect of supernatural marriage.

It must be said again that supernatural marriage is a gift from God, but it requires us to respond to His promptings in order for it to be experienced. If we resist what God is trying to do in our lives, we can stop God from working supernaturally in our marriages. Of course God is big enough that He doesn't need our permission to move in our lives, but He longs to be desired.

What might zeal look like in our marital relationships? When implanted in us by God, zeal empowers us to love our partners with passion and pursue life together with joyful enthusiasm. We have been joined together supernaturally so that we can minister together with Spirit-led effectiveness. Each of us treats the other with complete respect and total honor. We actively focus our lives in the quest to fully accomplish the destiny of our marital union. Individually and as one, we wholeheartedly seek righteousness and intimacy with God.

BURNING WITH PASSION

Undoubtedly, God wants your desire for Him and His plan to be *hot!* God calls us as His disciples to be extreme in our relationship with Him. Jesus said to the church of Laodicea, "I know your deeds, that you are neither cold nor hot. I wish you were either one or the other. So, because you are lukewarm - neither hot nor cold - I am about to spit you out of my mouth" (Revelation 3:15-16). We are called to unwavering faith, complete trust, enduring love, and absolute obedience to the Lord Jesus Christ. Jesus demonstrated all these qualities during His life as a man upon the earth. He showed extreme honor to the Father by immediately responding to everything the Holy Spirit asked Him to do. In responding to the Jews, Jesus said that "the Son can do nothing by himself; he can do only what he sees his Father doing, because whatever the Father does the Son also does" (John 5:19). Having a passionate desire for the things of God led Jesus into unprecedented and unexpected (by men) success with huge eternal consequences. The same kind of result can occur in you and in your marriage if you maintain a fervent desire for God.

Regardless of where you currently are in your marriage, even if you have not yet established a marriage, it is critically important that you aim for the complete fulfillment of what God has planned for you. It is not good to dispassionately accept imperfection, but neither is it helpful to be discouraged by it. You can confidently anticipate progress knowing your hope will not disappoint you (Romans 5:5). It is completely safe to trust in the promises of God. Through His presence, God will draw you into what is absolutely the best for you and your marriage. **It is His passionate desire that your marriage shine out the eternal glory of His Kingdom.**

SHINING GOD'S GLORY IN OUR LIVES AND MARRIAGES

The golden lampstand crafted for the tabernacle in Exodus 25 and seen as a vision in Zechariah 4 are described in the Bible to show us how our lives can shine the glory of the Lord. The angel asked Zechariah, "What do you see?" Zechariah answered, "I see a solid gold lampstand with a bowl at the top and seven lights on it, with seven channels to the lights. Also there are two olive trees by it, one on the right of the bowl and the other on its left" (Zechariah 4:1-2).

Keith Miller of Stand Firm World Ministries gives a wonderful teaching on these lampstands in his school, *The Sevenfold Spirit of God*. We and our marital relationships were created to be bright flames on golden lampstands, constantly shining the light of God's glorious presence in us.

In Leviticus 24:2 Moses was instructed, "Command the Israelites to bring you clear oil of pressed olives for the light so that the lamps may be kept burning continually." For its flame to never go out, the lampstand required an endless supply of fresh olive oil – hence the two olive trees dripping into it in Zechariah's vision.

As supernatural believers, we are filled and continually resupplied with the oil of anointing from God's Spirit. The fire of God's presence ignites the oil within us, producing an eternal flame and projecting brilliant light. This radiant light truly can shine forever because its source is God Himself.

When the glow of God's glory radiates from the center of our supernatural marriages, it overcomes the darkness that surrounds us. This is a magnificent response to Jesus' instruction in the Sermon on the Mount:

> You are the light of the world. A city on a hill cannot be hidden. Neither do people light a lamp and put it under a bowl. Instead they put it on its stand, and it gives light to everyone in the house. In the same way, let your light shine before men, that they may see your good deeds and praise your Father in heaven.   – Matthew 5:14-16

Along with the seven lamps of the lampstand described in the first tabernacle were its wick trimmers, which were also made of pure gold (Exodus 37:23). To keep an oil lamp burning brightly it is periodically necessary to trim off the black deposits that collect at the end of the wick. If the wicks are not trimmed they will eventually produce more smoke than flame, greatly diminishing their ability to produce light.

As "Christ's ambassadors" (2 Corinthians 5:20), it is essential that we represent Him well. Jesus is the "light of the world" (John 8:12) and John referred to Him as the light shining in the darkness (John 1:5). God is so full of light that "in him there is no darkness at all" (1 John 1:5), and He wants our whole body to be full of light as well (Luke 11:36) so that Christ's glory can be seen clearly radiating from within us. We cannot represent Jesus well, nor can we shine out His glorious light unless we obediently walk in holiness before Him. Proverbs 13:9 reminds us, "The light of the righteous shines brightly, but the lamp of the wicked is snuffed out."

Pure gold usually represents holiness throughout the Bible. We must request and allow God to use His golden wick trimmers to make us holy. He desires to remove all imperfection and impurity from our lives so that the flame burning within us will consistently produce dazzling light. God does not desire that we, individually or in our marriages, place our light under a bowl. Rather, He would have us place it on a stand for the world to see. Although the metaphor is different, the concept is the same as that of God's fire refining us to become the purest gold. Both brilliant flames and fine gold glow with glory. We can trust God's words spoken through King David in Psalm 34:5, and as sung so powerfully by Alberto and Kimberly Rivera, "Those who look to him are radiant; their faces are never covered with shame."[10]

During much of my life I was comfortable doing things which seemed to be in a morally gray zone – neither completely right nor definitely wrong. When driving I rationalized that it was acceptable to go a few miles per hour above the posted speed limit because police officers would not bother to pull me over for a ticket. Business decisions that were not completely honest were tolerable as long as they were not illegal and if no one else could possibly find out what was done. I seemed to be constantly drawn to look over the edge of the straight and narrow path to be sure I did not miss something important by being too obedient.

As I have learned to receive the incomprehensible love God has for me as His child, my heart has been purified and my desires transformed. When I was filled with God's love I was enabled to openly welcome His refining fire. More and more I have lost

---

[10]These lyrics are from a song called, "Taste and See" on an album entitled, *The Father Sings* by Alberto and Kimberly Rivera.

interest in the unholy things consumed by God's fire. The passion of my life is to clearly hear the voice of Holy God and obediently do exactly what He asks of me.

The glory of God really can shine out from our individual lives and marriages if we believe God's promises and allow Him to make us pure and holy. We cannot produce glory on our own. It can only come from His supernatural presence. If we become self-satisfied and prideful, God's glory within us will quickly fade. Impurity in our thoughts and motives, selfish ambition, and desire to control others will extinguish the flame and attenuate the light. The primary goal of our radiating God's glory must be exclusively to honor God.

GLORY TO OVERCOME

Many become discouraged because their spouses show little interest or belief in God. Others are married to partners who are faithful believers, but have not yet learned the value of intimately relating to the Lover of their souls. In these situations it is important to not underestimate the power and effectiveness of God's glory shining out from one's life on a daily basis. God has placed within every person an intense desire for His glory that is longing to be satisfied. Through one spouse the other can experience a small taste of God's indescribable goodness. An unbelieving husband "may be won over without words by the behavior of their wives" (1 Peter 3:1). Even one tangible perception of the God of the supernatural can forever change the perceiver.

You can be a godly spouse and a blessing to your family regardless of the current level of your partner's participation with God. Nothing can separate you from the love of God (Romans 8:38-39). Satan himself cannot prevent the river of God's love from flowing through you to all who know you. Of course it is harder when your spouse does not believe in the Lord, or is lukewarm with God. But the point is that all of that can be overcome.[11] The glory of God inside of you will ultimately triumph over the spirit of the world and every attack of the enemy that tries to come against you. Remember that you "are from God and have overcome ... because the one who is in you is greater than the one who is in the world" (1 John 4:4).

The glory of the Lord shining out from you can rekindle desire for God in others, including your spouse and children, regardless of how deeply their desire for Him may be hidden. You may rely on the fact that seeking first the Kingdom and righteousness of God will increase your ability to share His truth, love, and glory with all who know you. When you seek God you will find Him. His holy presence within you will supernaturally transform your ability to relate to others, particularly the partner with whom you have chosen to be one. Jesus said to "seek first his kingdom and his righteousness, and all these things will be given to you as well" (Matthew 6:33).

---

[11]See "Addendum" at the back of this book on practical ways to overcome and relate to an unbelieving or nominal spouse in a supernatural way: "Advice to Laura: How to Live When Unequally Yoked."

Chapter Nine

STYLES OF MARRIAGE:

BITTER, TOLERABLE, AND FUNCTIONAL MARRIAGE

lthough the entire range of marriage styles is broad and diverse, it is useful to look at the major categories of marriage to see where a relationship has been, where it presently is, and where it someday could be. Certainly many couples demonstrate elements of more than one variety of marriage, but most relationships will fit well into one of five styles. In this chapter I am going to explain three of the five styles of marriage and then in the next two chapters we are going to look at the fourth and fifth styles, namely an exemplary marriage and then go on to God's best for our marriages – a supernatural marriage.

For those who are already married, it is valuable to honestly evaluate how you and your spouse relate within the marriage. When looking at a complex map posted in a public area there is often a red arrow accompanied by the words, "YOU ARE HERE." Once you know where you are it is much easier to determine how to get to where you would like to be. It is the same in marital relationships. Knowing the truth of where you are is the first step toward becoming truly free. Jesus said, "You will know the truth, and the truth will set you free" (John 8:32). It is not the truth that sets you free, but *knowing* the truth is what really sets you free. If you don't know where you are in your marriage, how can you become free? You must be honest with yourself, your marriage, and ultimately with God so He can bring freedom into your life.

Do not be discouraged by areas of immaturity and imperfection you recognize in your marriage. There has never been a perfect marital relationship besides the one that existed before the fall between Adam and Eve. In the same vein, there is no marriage so flawed as to be beyond God's ability to improve. "We, who with unveiled faces all reflect the Lord's glory, are being transformed into his likeness with ever-increasing glory" (2 Corinthians 3:18). Transformation is a divine process which occurs over time. God is very pleased and quite able to advance you and your marriage into the realm of the supernatural. Our participation in this amazing and beautiful change leads to an increase in God's eternal glory.

In reality there are an infinite number of available styles of marriage. No two people are made exactly alike. As unique individuals join in marriage, each relationship has its own particular set of assets, liabilities, opportunities, and challenges. For simplicity's sake, the continuum of marital styles will be divided into five basic types. Let us begin with a lower level, barely functioning style of marriage and press on toward the goal God has set before us (Philippians 3:14).

Bitter Marriage

Bitter marriage is characterized by the dangerous and harmful interactions of spouses who are bound by self-centeredness, anger, and resentment. Each spouse is persistently unhappy and frequently contributes to the increasing misery of the other. This type of marital relationship is celebrated by modern society as humorous entertainment on television sitcoms, in funny movies, and through the perverse jokes of stand-up comedians. Satan uses the avenue of humor to sneak this damaging way of relating beneath the protective radar of our spiritual awareness. The true nature of bitter marriage is not funny at all. It is serious – potentially deadly to all involved.

One person treating another with extreme inappropriateness is at first painful to our understanding of what we know should be true within marriage. In real life, after we are repeatedly exposed to hurtful words and harmful actions between spouses, we are left with the difficult decision as to whether we should cry or laugh. With time it becomes more and more painful to cry. The powers of darkness want us to laugh at what is sent to destroy us. The writer of Proverbs reminds us, "Reckless words pierce like a sword" (12:18).

Humor is used in an attempt to disguise the noxious effects of this relationship style. Truly, there is nothing funny about bitterness in any marriage. Treating each other with suspicion, contempt, resentment and anger is extremely harmful to any relationship, especially the marital relationship. These ways of interacting damage the supporting structures of their individual lives, their family, society in general, and the bride of Christ.

God's design for marriage naturally leads to the development and enjoyment of the fruit of the Spirit (Galatians 5:22-23). The fact that bitterness is endemic to a relationship verifies that the fruit of the Spirit is rarely present or is missing altogether. When both partners participate in bitter marriage, the normal result is that their relationship will gradually spiral downward. With time the acts of the sinful nature become more and more evident in each spouse's life.

Perhaps the most prominent characteristic of those involved in bitter marriage is glaring selfishness, which is demonstrated by frequent attempts to manipulate and control others within the family. In fact, just as God's Spirit produces fruit, so having a bitter marriage is something Paul defines as an act of the sinful nature. He says, "The acts of the sinful nature are obvious: sexual immorality, impurity and debauchery; idolatry and witchcraft; hatred, discord, jealousy, fits of rage, selfish ambition, dissensions, factions and envy; drunkenness, orgies, and the like" (Galatians 5:19-21).

The spirit of antichrist inspires bitter marriage. It is full of deadly venom from the serpent himself. Without supernatural intervention, its destiny is the pit of hell. In its full-blown expression, bitter marriage is the antithesis of what holy matrimony was created to be in God's sight. It is extremely dangerous to those involved and all those who know them.

As discouraging as this might seem, there is always hope even for the most bitter of marriages. Noah lived during the most evil time in recorded history (Genesis 6:5). Yet, through his faith and obedience God miraculously brought salvation to Noah and his entire family (2 Peter 2:5). When Jesus lived on earth as the Messiah, He brought life to the dead in both the natural and supernatural realms. When the heart of even one spouse in a marriage is opened to receive the transforming love of God, what appears to be impossible becomes possible. What can result is no less amazing than the resurrection of Jesus Himself.

TOLERABLE MARRIAGE

The second style of marriage is the tolerable marriage. In an era when tolerance is worshiped as a primary virtue in our society, the tolerable marriage has become the most common style of marriage. This type of relationship is not the American dream, but actually is the American norm. A tolerable marriage can be viable enough to last a lifetime and can outwardly appear to be very strong. But at its foundation, it is unstable, unreliable, and barely surviving each crisis it encounters. Many of the crises experienced are actually caused by one or both spouses. The partners enjoy no real goal or shared purpose greater than trying to hold things together and put up with each other year after year. This marriage is not walking in God's best, but just living a normal, mediocre, fairly good life with each other.

This kind of marriage is held together for practical reasons and convenience. It is not based in a relationship with God and pays little attention to biblical principles. Interactions between the spouses are guided by values learned from secular teaching based in the natural realm. Husband and wife stay together and present a weakly united front for the sake of the children or to maintain financial stability. They are responding to what is left of societal pressure for couples to remain married. The partners have some mental and emotional commitment to marriage and family, but no real love relationship with each other and no true marital covenant. They are just putting up with each other day after day, year after year.

Interactions between partners in a tolerable marriage are rooted in spiritual immaturity and demonstrate a significant degree of self-centeredness. The spouses share little trust for one another due to a number of negative previous experiences. Each maintains an attitude toward the other which is neutral at best and often defaults to the baseline assumption that their partner's intentions are bad even when they are not. In fact, some of this mistrust may be earned.

Without the supernatural intervention of God's love and mercy, the tension caused by painful experiences of the past relentlessly build. Self-protective mechanisms within each spouse are activated by the powers of darkness leading to hardness, sarcasm, and extreme pessimism. The most eminent danger to the tolerable marriage is general discouragement that can lead to despair. With little hope for the future, each partner stays in the relationship only through sheer determination. Eventually physical and emotional strength can fatigue, allowing the relationship to slip backwards into deepening division.

The encouraging aspects of a tolerable marriage include the desire by spouses to establish and maintain something of significance. They have been held back by not understanding the eternally valuable goals for life and marriage, which are attainable for every individual. Although their relationship is far from ideal, they have made a significant commitment to the concept of marriage as demonstrated by their willingness to tenaciously hold on to their partner over time. Each has been willing to pursue something of worth that is beyond the limitations of self-interest. The fire may be only smoldering, but hope for a flame is still alive.

FUNCTIONAL MARRIAGE

A tolerable style of marriage, upgraded through the application of good quality human psychology and behavior modification, becomes a functional marriage. This is the ultimate goal of worldly thinking based in the natural realm. Functional relationships are indirectly supported through the use of concepts revealed to man in the words of the Bible. However, the supernatural wisdom is disguised and weakened by its secular interpretation.

This type of marriage is much more comfortable and stable than those previously described. In it the partners are significantly more other-centered, and each generally assumes their mate's intentions are good. The life these spouses share is not truly abundant, but there is much about it which is good. The spouses usually enjoy being together and their marriage functions smoothly while achieving many useful goals. Children in the family can feel secure because they believe their parents love each other. The marital relationship is usually enjoyable, productive, and mutually encouraging. Satisfaction can be regularly experienced, and hope for the future is based in reality.

Functional marriages tend to last many years. The partners really try to be nice to each other so there is no strong motivation to leave. If these spouses were discussing their relationship they might say, "We have made a good marriage for ourselves." The theme song of functional marriage would be, "I did it my way." The foundation of this type of marriage is human wisdom and its building is accomplished by the strength of man. The primary danger to a strong functional marriage is the growth of pride in the hearts of each person involved in the relationship.

Many couples have, through their own desire and effort, achieved what the world would consider to be a good marriage. Just as Jesus revealed the weakness of the church in Laodicea, the couples in this type of marriage need to realize where they are and the weaknesses they have:

> You say, "I am rich; I have acquired wealth and do not need a thing." But you do not realize that you are wretched, pitiful, poor, blind and naked. I counsel you to buy from me gold refined in the fire, so you can become rich; and white clothes to wear, so you can cover your shameful nakedness; and salve to put on your eyes, so you can see. – Revelation 3:17-18

In their minds they believe, "I am rich; I have acquired a good marriage and do not need a thing." What they have accomplished appears to be big in their own eyes. Although this is their own view, it actually blocks their view of what is much bigger, better, and even more glorious. A more excellent way is available to them, but not perceived. Pride based on the good that has been achieved can block progression to something considerably better.

There is, however, much that is praiseworthy in a functional marriage. It demonstrates desire for a committed relationship, willingness to work toward a laudable goal, and dedication to shared values. If these marriage partners will honestly pursue the will and the ways of God, they will naturally advance in the beauty of their love relationship together as well as the strength and stability of the entire family. Function is considerably better than dysfunction. Functional marriage is fertile soil for the growth of opportunity and hope.

While this form of marriage isn't bad in and of itself, there is still much further room to grow and mature. It is not as bad as the bitter marriage or even the tolerable marriage, but it still severely lacks God's desire and intention in the marriage covenant. Let us look at another style of marriage that is better than those previously mentioned, yet still not God's best – the exemplary marriage.

Chapter Ten ✳

Styles of Marriage: Exemplary Marriage

Functional marriage is a very good thing. However, for a marriage to be exemplary, the partners involved must know and apply behaviors taught in God's Word. Partners in exemplary marriage are strongly motivated to live in ways that fulfill God's plan. It is helpful for husbands and wives to have a mental understanding of what is instructed in the Bible, yet little is accomplished until biblical concepts are actually obeyed. This level of marriage requires genuine desire for and commitment to lordship as we discussed in Chapters Six and Seven. Acceptance of Jesus as Lord of our lives transforms how we relate to one another in marriage, making it truly exceptional. It is impossible to reach this level of marriage without the involvement of God, His Word, and His lordship over our lives. What are the characteristics of an exemplary marital relationship? I want us to look at four characteristics that can be found in any marriage that is exemplary.

LOVE

The first characteristic to be found in exemplary marriage is love. When asked by someone what the "greatest commandment in the Law" was, Jesus responded by saying: "'Love the Lord your God with all your heart and with all your soul and with all your mind.' This is the first and greatest commandment. And the second is like it: 'Love your neighbor as yourself.' All the Law and the Prophets hang on these two commandments" (Matthew 22:34-40).

Jesus tells us that loving our neighbor is just as important as loving God. Both are absolutely essential to understanding and accomplishing His will in the earth. As we learn to love God, He imparts to us the ability to love our neighbor as we love ourselves. We cannot fully love until God enables this ability in our hearts. There is no neighbor so great in significance or as close in proximity as a partner in marriage. So we greatly honor God when we honestly and consistently love our spouse.

From the beginning it has been God's desire that we "should love one another" (1 John 3:11). His will is no different now than it was in the Garden of Eden. Our ability to love, both in and beyond our marital relationship, is the primary indicator of the validity of our connectedness with God. The apostle John states this quite clearly:

> Dear friends, since God so loved us, we also ought to love one another. No one has ever seen God; but if we love one another, God lives in us and his love is made complete in us ... God is love. Whoever lives in love lives in God, and God in him.　　　　　　　　　　　　– 1 John 4:11-12, 16

When we are saved, the Holy Spirit enters us and lives inside of us. God Himself, who is love, actually exists within our spirits and love itself becomes a prominent part of who we are. The supernatural presence of God in us changes the desires of our hearts, altering the way we think, speak, and behave. Most importantly, the entrance of God into our very being enables us to live and dwell "in love." The transforming love of God regularly flows between partners as they relate with each other in exemplary marriage. This shared love is the same holy love God blesses each of us with as His treasured children. It is only the love we learn to receive from God that enables us to truly love our spouses the way God desires.

The New Testament writers use the Greek word *agape* to help explain the perfect love of God intended to flow through each person involved in marriage. This is the type of love described so beautifully and poetically in 1 Corinthians 13. In fact, by inspiring this glorious chapter defining *agape* love, God perfectly describes Himself. *Agape* love is the essence of who God is. It is the solid rock upon which holy matrimony is built. Paul writes:

> Love is patient, love is kind. It does not envy, it does not boast, it is not proud. It is not rude, it is not self-seeking, it is not easily angered, it keeps no record of wrongs. Love does not delight in evil but rejoices with the truth. It always protects, always trusts, always hopes, always perseveres.
>
> Love never fails.   – 1 Corinthians 13:4-8

Agape is selfless and giving. Its motives are completely pure. *Agape* looks to the needs and desires of others in relationship with us and it demonstrates patience and kindness while wrapping its possessor in a cloak of humility. One who is filled with *agape* forgives easily, enabling the release of injuries from the past with a fully open hand. A spouse filled with the *agape* of God maintains hope even in situations where logic would dictate despair, knowing we will not be disappointed by hope: "And hope does not disappoint us, because God has poured out his love into our hearts by the Holy Spirit, whom he has given us" (Romans 5:5).

The secular world celebrates *eros*, which is romantic and sensual love, as being of primary importance in establishing and maintaining a marital relationship. Although *eros* is extremely useful and enjoyable in the covenant of marriage, its status as being more essential to a good marriage than *agape* is based in idolatry. *Eros*, by itself, is an unreliable foundation upon which many marriages and families are built. It can be passionate and strong, but its intensity varies significantly over time. *Agape* is stable, reliable, and eternally valuable in all human relationships. It provides security to a marriage which is not threatened by the circumstances of life or the winds of time. When received as a gift from God, *agape* can be as unchanging as the Giver Himself.

A third word for love from Greek linguistics is *phileo*. This form implies the affectionate love shared between the closest of friends written about in Proverbs 18:24, "A man of many companions may come to ruin, but there is a friend who sticks closer than a brother." It is used to express shared fondness between two people who truly enjoy being together. *Phileo* can and should be strongly evident in the marital relationship. Ever since we met in the medical school library, Linda and I have each considered the other to be our dearest friend. There is no closer or more cherished friend than a godly spouse in an exemplary marriage.

The fourth type of love is *storgos*, which is a love that exists between family members. God has placed within each of us a particularly strong desire to remain connected to our earthly family. These relationships are so important they were included in the short list of the Ten Commandments etched in stone on Mt. Sinai: "Honor your father and your mother, so that you may live long in the land the Lord your God is giving you" (Exodus 20:12). Even secular society honors a particularly strong bond between family members as is demonstrated by the expression, "blood is thicker than water."

Agape, eros, phileo, and *storgos* are all clearly evident in an exemplary marriage. The consistent presence of all four kinds of love secures the couple's bond by providing joy, satisfaction, and stability. Each spouse feels completely loved and totally accepted by the other. It is God's desire that all His married children experience, within their union, every available aspect of a deep and rich love relationship.

HONOR

A second characteristic to those dwelling in an exemplary marriage is honor. Exemplary marriage becomes possible when both partners accept the complete lordship of God in their individual lives. Establishing lordship is an essential prerequisite for the successful pursuit of righteousness. The union of two people who honestly seek both righteousness and love creates a relational environment capable of producing an abundant and prosperous life together. Again, the writer of Proverbs states, "He who pursues righteousness and love finds life, prosperity and honor" (21:21). Honor is naturally expressed to one another within this type of marriage. The marital union also receives honor from family, friends, and God Himself.

Honor is similar to *agape* in that both must be conferred on one person by another. It is not possible to truly honor one's self. In Romans 12:10 Paul instructs us, "Honor one another above yourselves." In marriage we honor our spouse when, through our words or through our actions, we show them respect and esteem them higher than ourselves. Paul and Peter both write about the respect and honor we are to show each other in the body of Christ, and more specifically in marriage:

However, each one of you also must love his wife as he loves himself, and the wife must respect her husband.

– Ephesians 5:33

Husbands, in the same way be considerate as you live with your wives, and treat them with respect as the weaker partner and as heirs with you of the gracious gift of life, so that nothing will hinder your prayers.   – 1 Peter 3:7

Give everyone what you owe him: If you owe taxes, pay taxes; if revenue, then revenue; if respect, then respect; if honor, then honor.   – Romans 13:7

In discussions on marriage, Ephesians 5:33 is often quoted in support of the concept that a husband's primary responsibility is to love his wife while the most important thing a wife can do is to respect her husband. There is some validity to emphasizing differing roles for men and women as they relate to one another in marriage, but there is much more similarity than disparity when discussing spousal roles within true holy matrimony. Peter instructs husbands relating with their wives also to "treat them with respect," while every follower of Jesus owes respect and honor to others to whom it is due (Romans 13:7). This is pointedly true within the mutually encouraging relationship of exemplary marriage. In this aspect of the marital relationship, as with many others, there is neither "male nor female" (Galatians 3:28), but all are one in Christ Jesus.

In exemplary marriage both partners are intent on living godly lives which are worthy of respect. The directives written in 1 Timothy 3 are specific for the appointing of deacons in the church. However, there is nothing in these verses different from what God desires of all His children. Verse 8 says, "Deacons ... are to be men worthy of respect," while verse 11 says, "In the same way, their wives are to be women worthy of respect." Godly behavior is essentially the same regardless of gender, marital status, or specific calling in ministry. When we consistently live lives that honor God, it becomes natural and effortless for our spouses to sincerely admire and honor us.

Honor cannot be invented or manufactured; it requires some form of justification. Everyone can be respected and honored to some degree simply because they bear the likeness of God, however shabbily. Although godly actions make it much easier to bestow honor upon an individual, it is not necessary to delay the showing of respect until every aspect of a person's life is admirable. Virtually every spouse has qualities that can be revered and celebrated, and doing so is useful and encouraging to both partners in the relationship. Honor given and received by spouses brings remarkable depth, stability, and enjoyment to exemplary marriage.

COVENANT

Everlasting covenants were made between God and Noah, and later between God and Abraham. These were initiated and established entirely by God before either Noah or Abraham had the opportunity to participate in the accomplishing of His covenantal plan and purpose. These covenants had implications far beyond the understanding of either of these godly men and extended blessings to their descendents forever. A sign accompanied each covenant – the rainbow for Noah and the sign of circumcision for Abraham.

Similarly, exemplary marriages are based in a covenantal relationship, initiated and established by God, between Himself and the couple He has made to be one. This covenant is richer than words spoken in a ceremony, much deeper than strictly human commitment, and more binding than any contract written by the hand of man. A contract is immediately broken when either party involved fails to fulfill any aspect of the contractual obligation. The failures of Abraham's descendants did not destroy the eternal covenant made with them by our faithful God. In the same vein, imperfect actions, on the part of one or both marital partners, do not end the covenant relationship established by God. In exemplary marriage the covenant between man, woman, and God is maintained by all three parties involved. Nothing is capable of breaking this strong cord of three strands (Ecclesiastes 4:12).

Everlasting Covenant

When God made His covenants with Noah and Abraham, they had not yet accomplished any of the great things for which they would later be honored. In fact, they had little concept of what God's plans were or how they could be useful as participants in those plans. When man and woman enter a covenantal marriage, their desire to participate in God's purposes for them is honestly expressed, but their understanding of what this means is very incomplete. They are strangers in a foreign country, as was Abraham (Hebrews 11:9). Also, similar to Abraham, God has amazing plans for them and their relationship if they remain faithful and obedient. When God makes a covenant, He is consistently and astonishingly good to those who fear Him so that they will "never turn away." God declares, "I will make an everlasting covenant with them: I will never stop doing good to them, and I will inspire them to fear me, so that they will never turn away from me" (Jeremiah 32:40). So it is within the covenant of exemplary marriage.

Covenant of Love

God's covenantal promises made to Noah and Abraham extended to their descendants forever. He is no less willing or able to bless the descendants of those today who honor Him with love and faithful obedience. Love and lordship are the primary motivators in an exemplary marriage. With these consistently present, the covenant between God, man, and woman flourishes and is enabled to accomplish the purposes for which it is intended. In this type of a marriage, children are raised in a home where the love of God is experienced and His truths are revered. When the covenant of marriage is truly honored, God will extend his "covenant of love to a thousand generations." For Deuteronomy 7:9 declares, "Know therefore that the Lord your God is God; he is the faithful God, keeping his covenant of love to a thousand generations of those who love him and keep his commands." Through an exemplary marriage, your children and your children's children will be abundantly blessed.

Covenant of Peace

Another aspect of the covenant God establishes with us is peace. Linda and I have enjoyed a covenant of peace with each other and with God since the first day of our marriage. When friends enter our home for the first time, they often comment that they feel a calming sense of peace. I once thought this was something physically or spiritually unique about the property we own, but I now believe what they are experiencing is the covenant of peace given to us by God as we have honored His desires for us in our covenantal marriage. Isaiah prophesied, "'Though the mountains be shaken and the hills be removed, yet my unfailing love for you will not be shaken nor my *covenant of peace* be removed,' says the Lord, who has compassion on you" (54:10, *emphasis mine*). And God goes on to say through Ezekiel, "I will make a *covenant of peace* with them and rid the land of wild beasts so that they may live in the desert and sleep in the forests in safety" (34:25, *emphasis mine*).

Jesus says in Matthew 18:20, "For where two or three come together in my name, there am I with them." Jesus is the "Prince of Peace" (Isaiah 9:6), and if He is with the two of us as we live together in holy matrimony, then "the peace of God, which transcends all understanding" (Philippians 4:7) will be recognized by those who know us. Just as God's sign for Noah was the rainbow and His sign for Abraham was circumcision, I believe profound peace between and around a married couple is His sign to the world of their God-ordained, covenantal oneness. Because they have both received the Holy Spirit at salvation, partners in an exemplary marriage are fully able to "keep the unity of the Spirit through the bond of peace" (Ephesians 4:3).

SACRIFICE

Fulfilling the requirements of love, honor and covenant in exemplary marriage often requires true sacrifice, which is the fourth characteristic of an exemplary marriage. Although the specific details of the sacrifice required will vary for different couples, appropriate surrender of personal desires and plans is needed in every marital relationship. The surrender of individual wishes for another's needs to be fulfilled is an action based in the selflessness of the *agape* type of love.

In the context of marriage, Paul reminds husbands and wives to "Submit to one another out of reverence for Christ" (Ephesians 5:21). God expects us to demonstrate mutual submission as we deal with others within the bride of Christ. Sacrificial deference to the wishes of a spouse on a regular basis is critical to the development of love, trust, and respect between marital partners. In our marriage, Linda and I try to do nothing out of selfish ambition or vain conceit, but in humility consider each other better than ourselves (Philippians 2:3). Although sacrificial acts toward another person are never easy, they can be joyful and rewarding when carried out as an expression of true love.

Some of the most difficult sacrifices made in our life together have been related to church fellowship. Linda and I grew up in quite different denominational traditions. Although we knew what we had been taught, it was often difficult to explain why those teachings were eternally significant to us. Not surprisingly, the conflicting beliefs we tenaciously held on to were often difficult to support using Scripture. Prior to marrying we spent many hours together talking, praying, struggling, and crying till we came to an agreement in our understanding of what we thought to be the vitally significant, non-negotiable issues of faith in God.

When Linda and I were first married we decided it would be best for us if we planned to always attend the same church together. We considered which church we would go to as being a negotiable decision, believing that eventually God would lead us to a fellowship that would be the best place for both of us. Initially we chose to attend the denomination in which I had grown up. In accepting this decision, Linda chose to sacrifice things very dear to her heart – such as her preferred style of worship. She did this as a demonstration of love to me and, in reverence for Christ, as an act of submission to me as the spiritual leader of our family. What she did was led by the "Spirit of wisdom" (Isaiah 11:2). During our years of associating with this body of believers, Linda patiently allowed God to transform my way of relating to both Him and her. Our covenant of peace enabled her to remain content until God drew us as a couple into our next church fellowship.

The desire of my heart gradually became to know God, instead of knowing only about God. As others have said, I wanted to become acquainted with the God of Acts[12] and not just be familiar

[12]This is, of course, referring to the book of Acts.

with the acts of God. After eleven years of marriage I became increasingly aware that, although I knew much truth, my knowledge had not led me into freedom (John 8:32). It became clear to me that freedom could not be found except where the Spirit of the Lord was present (2 Corinthians 3:17). After a brief search, we were led to a church focused on seeking intimacy in spiritual relationship with God. Although we had no idea yet what this meant, we knew we wanted it!

Linda had sacrificially submitted her desires to mine for years. We both sacrificed many things in our transition to a different church fellowship. My parents understood neither the reasons for the change, nor did they approve of the church we moved to. To make things even harder, we still had close, dearly loved friends at the church we were leaving. Most were very kind to us, but pain was evident on their faces and deeply felt within all of our hearts as we left. However, as is always the case, sacrifice in response to God's leading produces a bountiful harvest. Through mutual submission and joint sacrifice, our relationships with God, our marriage, and our children were all blessed through this pivotal transition.

A sacrificial act made to your spouse in marriage demonstrates a willingness to die to self and lay down your life for your dearest earthly friend. It is an *agape* love-filled response reminiscent of Jesus' ultimate sacrifice on the cross. In reference to the greatest act of all, Jesus said, "Greater love has no one than this, that he lay down his life for his friends" (John 15:13). This act of submission communicates honor and respect, which can be easily understood and strengthens the three-way covenant within the relationship. It clearly demonstrates to the world that marriage involving two partners committed to loving and serving God is truly exemplary.

SUMMARY

We have quickly explored the first four types of marital relationships. Bitter marriage is rooted in ungodly and dangerous ways of dealing with one another in an intimate relationship. Although quite weak and unpredictable, tolerable marriage demonstrates signs of life, hope, and a greater desire for the marriage to survive. Functional marriage is seen as satisfactory when judged by worldly standards. It is stable and comfortable for the marital partners, yet its potential is limited because it is built upon the wisdom and understanding of men.

Exemplary marriage far surpasses the other three types, because it can be entered only by spouses who have both knowledge of God's plan for relationships and true desire to follow Him as Lord of their lives. This kind of marriage is extremely enjoyable to both marital partners and a blessing to their family. Within it there can be great pleasure in experiencing every aspect of the safe playground of the marriage covenant. However, very real danger persists even in marriages that are amazingly good.

An exemplary marriage can be so enjoyable that the spouses become fully satisfied with their present situation. Satisfaction can lead to complacency, which is the ultimate enemy of spiritual and marital growth. Regardless of how good a marriage might be, we should not assume it is all God intends for us in our marital relationships. We should never stop asking for more of what God has for us, for He gives "good gifts to those who ask him" (Matthew 7:11). Linda and I continue to daily ask, seek, and knock for those good gifts. We have been surprised and amazed at God's responses to our seeking His Kingdom first (Matthew 6:33).

The God-centered, exemplary marriage of two faithful and obedient believers is as good as anyone could expect a relationship to be until the Holy Spirit adds the unexpected – the realm of the supernatural. We now move on to the unpredictable and astonishing realm of supernatural marriage in order to define what it is and recognize the blessings it provides for all involved.

Chapter Eleven

STYLES OF MARRIAGE: SUPERNATURAL MARRIAGE

W hen the supernatural invades the natural realm, the result is always miraculous. The miracle of salvation awaits those who are lost. The sick have the opportunity to receive the blessing of miraculous healing when the supernatural realm invades our natural realm. Likewise, spouses involved in any type of marital relationship can have their lives transformed through the miracle of supernatural marriage. Even an exceptional marriage can be catapulted to new levels of intimacy, joy, and productivity through consistent connection with God's supernatural realm.

The word "super" means to be above, over, or beyond. The supernatural realm is literally above or beyond the natural realm. It frees our natural bodies and souls to participate in things beyond what we normally consider possible. Marriage, as created by God, is incredibly enjoyable and good. The supernatural presence of the Holy Spirit in a marriage enables us to receive full benefits from this critically important part of our lives. Our otherwise unimaginable dreams and unachievable goals become fully available when God lives at the center of our marital relationships. His supernatural presence gives us access to the glory and power which exist in the throne room of heaven.

Two Factors Must be Present: Intimacy and Lordship

When Jesus was asked what was the greatest commandment, He responded with not one, but two answers. He said that the greatest commandment was to love God first, and secondly, to love our neighbor just as we love ourselves (Matthew 22:34-40). Similarly, supernatural marriage requires two concurrent realities for it to exist in the way God created it to exist. It cannot occur and cannot continue when only one of the two is present.

Intimacy, the welcomed presence of the Holy Spirit, is the first essential and defining characteristic of supernatural marriage. "God is spirit" (John 4:24), and our only direct connection to Him is spirit to Spirit in the realm of the supernatural. We have no way to effectively participate in this realm without His Spirit within us, leading us and empowering us to accomplish His purposes in the earth. Immanuel literally means, "God with us" (Matthew 1:23). Certainly, supernatural marriage demands that "Immanuel" be a reality in the marriage relationship. However, there is certainly more that is required for supernatural marriage to exist.

The second necessary feature of supernatural marriage is the consistent submission of both partners to Jesus as Lord. This lordship is demonstrated over time by obedience and faithfulness in fulfilling God's expectations and commands. As is expressed in the parable of the talents, our faithfulness to God and His ways makes Him happy. Because the servant was faithful to his master while he was away, the master replied to him, "Well done, good and faithful servant! You have been faithful with a few things; I will put you in charge of many things. Come and share your master's happiness!" (Matthew 25:21). Then Jesus confirms this at the end of the parable by saying: "For everyone who has will be given more, and he will have an abundance" (Matthew 25:29).

God is pleased to give His obedient children more and more until their lives are filled with abundance. So it is in supernatural marriage. As we are faithful to God and His ways in our marriages, He longs to give us more and more until our lives and marriages are abundantly full of His blessings and His presence.

Either lordship or intimacy with the Holy Spirit can be present first. The other can be added at a later time. The order of which one is first is not critical, but they must coexist for marriage to become fully what God intends it to be. Regardless of which characteristic is the first to be attained, the addition of the second releases the marriage to its ultimate destiny. This is very similar to a biological condition referred to as symbiosis.

Symbiosis occurs when two different types of organisms come together to create a life form which is much more productive and resilient than either organism on its own. Both organisms benefit from intimate relationship with the other. An example of this is lichen, created from the symbiotic combination of algae and fungus. Fungi obtain water and minerals, using them to form a protective shell around the algae. Algae use photosynthesis to produce food for both organisms. Although neither can survive for long alone, together they establish a mutualistic marriage which gives them strength to endure harsh and challenging conditions, but this is only possible as they work together.

In some ways supernatural marriage is akin to symbiosis. On one hand, marital partners focused on lordship alone honor God, but lack the gifting and power needed to function at a supernatural level in the Kingdom of God. On the other hand, spouses concentrating only on spiritual connectedness with God often fail to demonstrate consistent obedience to God and to what He has asked of them. This cripples their effectiveness in ministry and damages the integrity of Christ's bride.

Only when both are present concurrently does spiritual symbiosis occur. Bringing lordship and spiritual intimacy together in a marriage creates a new type of marital relationship which is incredibly strong, healthy, effective, and full of life. Gifting is abundant, supernatural power is available, the Kingdom of God is advanced, and great glory is brought to the King.

Not Satisfied

In our personal experience, the transition to supernatural marriage began with the issue of who was Lord of our lives. I believe this to be the most common pattern for those pursuing marriage in the supernatural realm. As I shared previously,[13] God did not allow me to even meet Linda until my inner desire for Jesus to be Lord had been earnestly confessed and securely established within my heart. Linda had been solidly connected with God for many years prior to our meeting in that library. Lordship was already an established, integral part of her life.

Through courtship and twenty-five years of marriage, our commitment to honor and obey the desires of God continued to increase. There were areas of disobedience which had to be uncovered and destroyed. God is always faithful to reveal what is not from Him if we truly desire to know - He longs for us to change

---

[13]I share this story of my development of Jesus becoming Lord of my life before meeting Linda in Chapter 6, "Savior, but Lord?" under the subtitle "An Important Lesson."

even more than we desire to change. Little by little we grew in our recognition of God's glorious goodness and the beauty and wisdom of His plan. We became more aware of His desire that we serve Him together as one flesh, as well as His ability to transform the way we relate to each other and to Him. In every way that we could comprehend at the time, Jesus had become Lord of both our lives and our marriage.

By our silver anniversary we had an exemplary marriage. We recognized that life with God was very good. Yet, a silent urge within drove both of us to not be fully satisfied with what we had. Linda and I enjoyed a wonderful and intimate oneness together, but recognized that something of great importance was still missing in our individual and marital relationships with God. We didn't want to settle for good because we somehow sensed we were not walking in God's best for us.

Not knowing where else to go, we cried out to God to fulfill what was missing in our lives and in our marriage. We expressed our love to Him, our desire to be fully faithful to Him, and our craving to receive everything available to those who believe. We verbally committed to God, friends, and family that we were "going for it" during the second half of our lives. Both of us were intent on fully submitting to God all that we had in every possible way. I believe verbalizing spiritual commitments to both God and those we know adds much strength to these pledges. Declarations release the destiny of our silent inner thoughts, revealing our intentions and expressing our authority in the natural and supernatural realms. The spoken word is powerful and effective. We overcome Satan not only "by the blood of the Lamb," but also "by the word of [our] testimony" (Revelation 12:11), and that testimony must be spoken in audible language.

THE POINT OF NO RETURN

The process of growing in supernatural connectedness with God can be found in the analogy of the way an airplane takes off from an airport – as a private pilot for twenty years, I am very familiar with this process. At the beginning of the runway, the pilot sets the engines at full throttle and begins a gradual acceleration to flight speed. Further down the runway there is a point at which the pilot must decide to abort the takeoff or commit the plane and all its occupants to flight. Once past this point the plane is committed to fly. It is no longer possible to safely stay on the ground or come to a stop before the runway ends. Just seconds after passing the point of no return the plane surges into the air. It finally experiences flight, the very purpose for which it was designed and built.

Many believers, like Linda and me, spend years of their lives truly wanting to fly with God but not knowing how. They make great progress as they accelerate down the runway of life, yet never attain enough velocity to leave the ground. At some point in most of our lives we reach the place where the eternally significant decision has to be made whether to accelerate and commit to flight or to hesitate, decelerate, and eventually abort the attempt to attain that for which we were created.

It is our destiny to "soar on wings like eagles" (Isaiah 40:31). Flying with God in the supernatural realm is an exhilarating experience which expands our capacity to participate in His glorious Kingdom. However, we must not despise the time spent, prior to flight, accelerating in our relationship with Him. Before this promise of flight, Isaiah reminds us that it is only "those who *wait* on the Lord" that "renew their strength." It is those who wait upon Him that are the ones who "shall mount up with wings like eagles" (Isaiah 40:31, NKJV, *emphasis mine*). This time of waiting and hoping is vitally important to our flight process. In my life these were the years God used to grow my faith and mature my understanding of Him and His ways. They were the years where God established Himself as Lord of all.

The commitment we made and shared with those we love was, for us, the point of no return. We had obligated ourselves to give the Holy Spirit access to every part of who we were. If we were to fly with God, Jesus had to be Lord of every aspect of our beings. This lordship must encompass not only our spirits and souls, but our bodies as well.[14] He is Lord of all and all of who we are must be in submission to Him.

After this commitment, things began to happen at an astonishingly rapid pace. Shortly after our pledge, God placed the wind of His Spirit beneath our wings. We flew freely for the first time in our lives in a way that was effortless. At the same time, experiencing the incredible, even tangible presence of God was so joyful and life giving, it made us desire Him all the more. Once in the air our goal together became to proceed to our supernatural destiny.

Our transition into the supernatural realm took place at the *Texas Ablaze* conference.[15] At that series of meetings, many of the encounters Linda and I had with the Holy Spirit occurred simultaneously. It was clear to the both of us that God was communicating to us together as one flesh, not only to us as individuals. What God was trying to say He was speaking to *us*, as a team and as partners. We had always placed extreme value on being one in our marital relationship prior to this conference. But that day God placed an exclamation mark on the significance of oneness as He lovingly arranged for us to experience Him in unison.

---

[14]This is further explained in Chapter 7, "Complete Lordship: Letting God Reign in Spirit, Soul, and Body."

[15]See Chapter 4, "Texas Ablaze: Our Journey into Supernatural Encounters with God."

For years our primary desire in life had been to individually and corporately establish Jesus as Lord. But that day was unique and transformational. It was eternally significant. As one flesh, God tangibly touched us - spirit, soul, and body - by His Spirit. For Linda and me, this was the point of transition into supernatural marriage.

SUPERNATURAL MARRIAGE: THE MORE EXCELLENT WAY

I was with Linda the day she heard "Holy is fun!" while swimming laps in the YMCA pool.[16] Swimming beside her that day, I too had asked God to give me revelation of what to speak forth that night concerning the subject of supernatural marriage. What I heard was this: "The principles, precepts, and performance of great (exemplary) marriage become presence, passion, and power in supernatural marriage." What an exhilarating experience it was for both of us when we, again as one flesh, had ears to hear the wisdom of God and what He would have us to speak about that night at the conference!

Supernatural marriage is not a one-time event. It is a way of life. Within it we relate to each other and to God in ways which are led more by the Holy Spirit and less by human understanding. The transition into the supernatural realm can be intimidating to many of us. It can also be confusing and disruptive of previous life plans. The result of the change, however, is well worth the struggles experienced en route.

Principles, Precepts, and Performance of Exemplary Marriage

Marriage that primarily exists within the natural realm can be satisfying and good. It can be functional[17] by conforming to

---

[16] See Chapter 1, "Holy Is Fun!" for a further explanation of this whole revelation to our hearts.

[17] See Chapter 9 on "Styles of Marriage: Bitter, Tolerable, and Functional Marriage" for a more complete definition of these types of marriage.

the teachings of men and can become truly exemplary[18] when it is structured around the written Word of God. Following God's *precepts* and the application of His *principles* requires *performance* to carry them out. Even non-believers who try to live their lives in accordance with what God teaches will be blessed just by following what is laid out in Scripture.

In using the word *principles*, I refer to the overriding concepts expressed in the Bible, of how to effectively and successfully relate to others. They include sound and valuable instruction such as, "Do to others what you would have them do to you" (Matthew 7:12); "Let your gentleness be evident to all" (Philippians 4:5); "To love your neighbor as yourself is more important than all burnt offerings and sacrifices" (Mark 12:33), and "wounds from a friend can be trusted" (Proverbs 27:6). These principles, while useful in any type of relationship, are pointedly applicable to the close and long term association of marriage.

David wrote of the principles and precepts of the Lord in this way:

The law of the Lord is perfect, reviving the soul.

The statutes of the Lord are trustworthy, making wise the simple.

The precepts of the Lord are right, giving joy to the heart.

The commands of the Lord are radiant, giving light to the eyes.

The fear of the Lord is pure, enduring forever.

The ordinances of the Lord are sure and altogether righteous.

They are more precious than gold, than much pure gold; they are sweeter than honey, than honey from the comb. By

---

[18]See Chapter 10 on "Styles of Marriage: Exemplary Marriage" for a definition of what exemplary marriage is.

them is your servant warned; in keeping them there is great
reward.   – Psalm 19:7-11

The precepts are the commands of God which prescribe the
specific and correct ways we should respond to the circumstances
experienced in life. For simplicity's sake, I am using this single
word to include the nuances of definition variation for the similar
words: law, statutes, commands, and ordinances. In Psalm 19 they
are described as perfect, trustworthy, right, and radiant – they are
more precious than gold and sweeter than honey.

God has immeasurably blessed us through His precepts recorded in the Bible. Although viewed by the world as unnecessary and
maddening constraints, the laws of God actually free us to enjoy
abundant life by providing boundaries within which we can safely
live.[19] Obediently following them gives us the stable structure of
life required for us to fulfill our destiny. Godly living is an absolute
prerequisite to a peaceful and satisfying marriage.

Accomplishment is the goal of *performance*. The ultimate value
of what is accomplished is usually determined by the way in which
it is achieved. We can attempt to please God by performing in a
manner that is consistent with human understanding of His principles and precepts. Yet, when our efforts are supported only by
our own abilities and strength, the result is of little or no eternal
value. The accomplishments produced by our performance will fully honor God only when they are initiated by the Spirit of wisdom
and achieved by the Spirit of power (Isaiah 11:2).

Performing the biblical duties of a husband or wife strictly within the natural realm can lead to an exemplary marital relationship.
However, partners in these marriages will never be able to fully

---

[19]Refers to Chapter 1, "Holy Is Fun!" and the blessings that can be received
living inside of God's boundaries and the consequences of living outside of His
boundaries.

experience oneness with each other, which requires supernatural connection, nor can they accomplish all of the eternal purposes for which their union was established. His ways are higher than ours (Isaiah 55:9), and fulfilling the divine plan God has for marriage requires complete lordship and capabilities beyond the limitations of the natural realm. To achieve the full destiny of marriage we must receive gifting that is only supernaturally available by God's power and might. We need the presence, passion, and power of God if we are to walk in supernatural marriage.

Presence, Passion, and Power of Supernatural Marriage

The abiding *presence* of the Holy Spirit in us provides us with supernatural comprehension of God's eternal and unchanging principles. Instead of these principles being lofty concepts we try to understand with our minds, they become patterns deposited in our hearts which draw us into ways of living that honor God. The Spirit makes us aware of our spouse's innermost needs and gives us insight into the best ways to bless them. Through God's glorious presence in us, His manifold wisdom will be made known as it manifests in and through our marriages. The presence of God in man is the primary requirement for all that we hope to achieve in His supernatural realm.

God's love for us is replete with *passion*, so much so that when Mel Gibson produced the movie about God's greatest demonstration of love, he named it *The Passion of the Christ*. As God pours out His love into our hearts by the Holy Spirit (Romans 5:5), His passion also pours into our lives. This passion is seen repeatedly in the lives of men and women connected with God during biblical times and the two thousand years since Jesus was physically present upon the earth.

Passion drives us to relentlessly pursue what we believe to be important. When led by the Spirit of God, we recognize both the present and the eternal significance of our most intimate human relationships. The feelings between marital partners, the physical desire to be with each other, and their demonstrations of love to one another, will all be marked by intense passion when God is consistently present at the center of their union. Just obeying the precepts of God is a good thing, but it becomes delight as we are motivated by passion. In supernatural marriage it is not out of drudgery or obligation that we obey God's command to love our spouse. Through the indwelling presence of God's love within us, we are motivated to passionately demonstrate love to the person with whom we are one. All of a sudden, in supernatural marriage, our duty becomes our delight.

With God's presence also comes His *power.* A couple whose marriage has entered the supernatural sphere does not only experience oneness within the relationship, but they actually become one in spirit with God. The transformation into oneness with God described in John 17:21[20] is not only available to the individual believer. I believe it also applies to those involved in marriage as well as to Christ's bride as a whole. When we are truly in unity with God, His power can and will be demonstrated in our lives.

In supernatural marriage, the power of God appears in many different ways. God's glorious power can be literally felt in human flesh. At times, enough of it enters our bodies that normal control and function are lost. This response is described by Ruth Ward

---

[20] Jesus prayed: "That all of them may be one, Father, just as you are in me and I am in you. May they also be in us so that the world may believe that you have sent me" (John 17:21).

Heflin as "falling into greatness."[21] When the Spirit of Jesus is in us, we possess a small portion of His Spirit of power described in Isaiah 11:2. This power can be shared with your spouse and with others by impartation through the laying on of hands.[22] Couples ministering together can use God's power in ways orchestrated by the Spirit of God to accomplish miraculous things for His glory in the areas of healing, deliverance, signs, and wonders.

New Levels and Greater Satisfaction

As a college student majoring in chemistry I learned about the structure and function of atoms. Electrons orbit around the nucleus of each atom at nearly the speed of light, forming energy shells. Within the shells are levels characterized by higher and lower degrees of energy. When a quantum of energy is applied to the atom, one electron is transferred to a higher state of energy. This sudden change is referred to as a quantum leap. The capacity of the atom to interact with its surroundings is greatly enhanced through the quantum leap caused by the addition of pure energy.

When we welcome and receive an increased indwelling of God's Spirit, it is as if a tiny portion of His power is deposited within the substance of our being. This is similar to a quantum of energy being added to the electron of an atom. The spiritual energy within us is dramatically increased, and our ability to accomplish amazing things is enhanced. The addition of power from God through connectedness with the Holy Spirit results in a quantum leap in our

---

[21] Ruth Ward Heflin, *River Glory*, (Hagerstown, MD: McDougal Publishing, 1999), 133. The entire quote is as follows: "If people could only realize that when they are slain in the Spirit they are falling into greatness, surely they would fall down more often."

[22] A biblical doctrine of the laying on of hands for the impartation of the Holy Spirit is found in passages such as, but not limited to, Hebrews 6:1-3; Numbers 11:16-18; Deuteronomy 34:9; 1 Timothy 4:14, 5:22; Mark 6:5, 8:23-25; Luke 4:40, 13:13-14; Acts 8:14-17, 19:6-7, 28:8; Romans 1:11-12.

ability to accomplish the will of God in our daily lives. His power conveys to us and our marriages new levels of effectiveness, satisfaction, and oneness which were previously unobtainable.

SUMMARY

I want to share with you another good analogy that comes from the lasers used in my work as an ophthalmologist. Naturally occuring light is composed of somewhat random waves of light which scatter quickly and have very limited power. This kind of light is referred to as incoherent because of its lack of pattern and organization. What makes laser light special is that it is coherent, which means that the waves are organized with wave peaks occurring at the same location at the same time. This tightly controlled focusing of the light makes it powerful and effective. Surgical procedures such as LASIK demonstrate to us how lasers can accomplish tasks that were unimaginable until we learned how to make light coherent.

Incoherent Light   Coherent Light

When the presence, passion, and power of God's Spirit are added to the bright light of exemplary marriage it becomes the laser light of supernatural marriage. As marital partners learn to obediently respond to each wave of the Holy Spirit, they function together with focus, coherence, and great power. In the supernatural realm spouses become able to accomplish things they previously had not even dreamed would be possible.

As we accept more of God's supernatural presence and allow His power to be activated within us, there is tremendous increase in our capacity, individually and in marriage, to accomplish eternally significant tasks. We are also supernaturally enabled to relate to our spouses in a different and more effective way than ever before. The purpose of it all is to bring great honor and glory to God.

We have seen what supernatural marriage is and how both intimacy with the Holy Spirit and Jesus being Lord of our lives must be present for supernatural marriage to be implemented in our lives. If we are expecting to live from and in the supernatural realm, then we must learn to be connected to the Source of the supernatural realm, who is God. And we must learn to obey what He commands of us.

God longs to take us from the drudgery of obeying the precepts of God out of duty, to the freedom of enjoying His presence, passion and power. It is as we experience God on a supernatural level that we will also be able to relate to our spouses on a supernatural level. Let us now look at the effects of what living in a supernatural marriage will have on us if we begin to press into God to know what He would have us do.

Chapter Twelve

THE EFFECTS OF SUPERNATURAL MARRIAGE

The entrance of Linda's and my marriage into the supernatural realm has allowed us to experience many things beyond the limits of what we assumed to be possible. When we were baptized in the river of the Holy Spirit, our perspectives on both temporal and eternal things changed. Like so many before us, we have learned and have repeatedly been reminded that with God all things are truly possible (Matthew 19:26).

Linda and I have been no less transformed than the crippled beggar healed by Peter at the temple gate called Beautiful (Acts 3:1-10). What I have I give to you in the sharing of our supernatural experiences, which have amazed, blessed, and encouraged us in our marriage and ministry. Here are a few of the effects of a supernatural marriage that Linda and I have been blessed with since coming into this revelation of what is possible with God in marriage.

SUPERNATURAL MINISTRY

The day we returned home from the *Texas Ablaze* conference[23] in Dallas, our pastor, Bob Beaver, sensed the change that had occurred in us and immediately asked us to be involved, as a couple, in the ministry of inner healing and deliverance. That very night we spent several hours praying with a man struggling with intense anger and unforgiveness. Two days later we did the same with a young woman plagued with fear and sexual sin. We had much to learn in getting started in this form of ministry, yet the glory and love of God accomplished amazing things in spite of us. In both situations we could clearly see freedom gained and maintained through deliverance from demonic control.

From time to time we can now sense in the spirit that one of us is suffering oppression during attacks from the kingdom of darkness. It is wonderfully convenient that each of us has a spouse who carries the authority and power made available to us by the Spirit of God. With a few declarations of truth and a brief time of focused prayer we are able to defeat the enemy's assault on our partner in its early stages before a stronghold can be established.

Just like the process of symbiosis mentioned previously, Linda and I have observed many situations where dramatically more can be accomplished when we work together as a team than when we labor alone. We have found the same to be true when others have shared their spiritual dreams with us and asked for interpretation. It is surprising how often the Holy Spirit will give each of us understanding of different aspects of the dream. Linda will be told the correct placement of some pieces of the puzzle while I receive

---

[23]See Chapter 4, "Texas Ablaze: Our Journey into Supernatural Encounters with God" for more information about our experiences with God during that conference.

revelation concerning the other parts. Either of us alone could be helpful in discovering the pieces, but together, the puzzle is solved.

It is very convenient, comfortable, and effective to minister together as a couple. We truly are one in the realm of the spirit. This connectedness enables us to naturally flow in and out of shared spiritual confrontations as if we were tag team wrestlers for God. Many times we are called to be in ministry apart from each other, but we relish the times it is possible to serve together. A marriage marked by supernatural oneness, where the husband, wife, and God are all in unison, can accomplish wondrous things in ministry for the glory of the Lord.

SUPERNATURAL PEACE

Three weeks later, while still taking our first steps together in supernatural marriage, Linda and I were driving on an icy highway in Wyoming. We were listening to a recording from the *Texas Ablaze* conference of Bill Johnson speaking about the time Jesus slept in a boat with His disciples while a squall raged about them on the Sea of Galilee (Luke 8:22-25). Although the disciples were frightened, Jesus maintained complete peace in the midst of the storm. His rebuking and calming of the storm demonstrated Jesus' authority – a miracle performed so the disciples could also be at peace. Bill said that we have authority in any storm of life in which we maintain supernatural peace.

Moments after we had for the second time heard this revelation, our SUV suddenly twisted out of control on black ice. We went off the road and across the median at full highway speed. As the vehicle slipped sideways it rolled four and a half times before finally coming to rest on its roof.

Amazingly, as the accident unfolded before our eyes and our bodies were violently beaten against the SUV's interior, Linda and I experienced a sense of profound peace. Earlier that month in Dallas, we had both felt the tangible touch of God's supernatural love that had driven out fear from within us (1 John 4:18). So we were prepared when this incident happened. What was inside of us automatically came out because of such a supernatural peace that resided within our hearts.

Although I was injured, no hospitalization was required. Linda had emergency abdominal surgery on Christmas Eve for a tear in her small intestine. Despite all of the injuries, twice during her week in the hospital Linda was blessed with angelic visitations. Other miraculous things occurred during a challenging journey as we left the blizzard conditions and returned to our home in Texas. Through it all we maintained constant, supernatural peace because God had granted us authority over this storm of life. Having peace in that situation would have never happened before we began to learn about living in the supernatural realm together. It was only because we had been growing in our understanding of the supernatural realm and what it means for our marriage that we could exude supernatural peace that passed our natural inclinations and understanding.

SUPERNATURAL PRESENCE AND MANIFESTATIONS

The next spring Amy Beth Beaver, the daughter of our pastor, returned to Texas after her first year at Bethel School of Supernatural Ministry. Linda and I spent two hours with her sharing the things she and we had recently learned concerning intimacy with God. At the close of our joyful discussion we asked her to pray for us. As she began to pray, Amy Beth thanked God for the things she had received from the Holy Spirit. She then laid one of her hands on each of our shoulders and very simply asked God to give to us everything she had received. It was a wonderful and encouraging time of prayer.

I felt nothing remarkable at the time, but Linda responded almost immediately with her head laid back and her body slumping down into the couch beside me. Although I was slightly disappointed to not have such an extraordinary experience with the presence of the Holy Spirit, I loved observing my wife respond to a touch from God. As we headed off toward our bedroom that evening, Linda and I discussed how we valued spending time with such precious friends – Amy Beth and the Holy Spirit.

Our tradition is to pray with each other every night just before we go to sleep. Praying together used to be awkward and uncomfortable for us, but after entering supernatural marriage it has become our favorite daily event that we look forward to every night. That particular night, Linda placed her hand on my chest as she prayed, imparting to me the gifts she had earlier received from the Holy Spirit. As she prayed, my body reacted with strong abdominal contractions and movements I chose not to control. I could feel the holy presence of God deep within my flesh. There was no doubt in my mind Linda had shared with me the same experience of God's glory she had received from Amy Beth.

For several minutes I lay motionless on the bed, basking in the precious peace only available in God's manifest presence. Then the Spirit of power rose up within me and I touched Linda's forehead with my hand, inviting the Holy Spirit to fill her with more and more of His glory. We prayed like this with each other for some time that night until our bodies were nearly exhausted.

During the following weeks we were compelled almost nightly to give and receive the presence and perception of God's Holy

Spirit. Recognition of His interaction with us would come at some times as a gentle touch; at others it would arrive as a series of intense waves. On a few occasions these ecstatic bodily sensations would suddenly and simultaneously come upon us both with no spoken word or particular action required on either of our parts. What we experienced during this remarkable period of time is reminiscent of something Charles Finney wrote in his autobiography over one hundred years ago:

> And as I closed the door and turned around, my heart seemed to be liquid within me. All my feelings seemed to rise and flow out; and the utterance of my heart was, "I want to pour my whole soul out to God." The rising of my soul was so great that I rushed into the room back of the front office, to pray.

> There was no fire, and no light, in the room; nevertheless it appeared to me as if it were perfectly light. As I went in and shut the door after me, it seemed as if I met the Lord Jesus Christ face to face. It did not occur to me then, nor did it for some time afterward, that it was wholly a mental state. On the contrary, it seemed to me that I saw him as I would see any other man. He said nothing, but looked at me in such a manner as to break me right down at his feet. I have always since regarded this as a most remarkable state of mind; for it seemed to me a reality, that he stood before me, and I fell down at his feet and poured out my soul to him. I wept aloud like a child, and made such confessions as I could with my choked utterance. It seemed to me that I bathed his feet with my tears; and yet I had no distinct impression that I touched him, that I recollect.

> I must have continued in this state for a good while; but my mind was too much absorbed with the interview to recollect

anything that I said. But I know, as soon as my mind became calm enough to break off from the interview, I returned to the front office, and found that the fire that I had made of large wood was nearly burned out. But as I turned and was about to take a seat by the fire, I received a mighty baptism of the Holy Ghost. Without any expectation of it, without ever having the thought in my mind that there was any such thing for me, without any recollection that I had ever heard the thing mentioned by any person in the world, the Holy Spirit descended upon me in a manner that seemed to go through me, body and soul. I could feel the impression, like a wave of electricity, going through and through me. Indeed, it seemed to come in waves and waves of liquid love for I could not express it in any other way. It seemed like the very breath of God. I can recollect distinctly that it seemed to fan me, like immense wings.

No words can express the wonderful love that was shed abroad in my heart. I wept aloud with joy and love; and I do not know but I should say, I literally bellowed out the unutterable gushings of my heart. These waves came over me, and over me, and over me, one after the other, until I recollect I cried out, 'I shall die if these waves continue to pass over me.' I said, 'Lord, I cannot bear any more;' yet I had no fear of death.[24]

The times in which we experienced these strong abdominal muscle contractions were generally followed by long periods of complete peace which are difficult to describe in words. Sometimes we explain these inexplicable responses to the Holy Spirit as, "speaking in tongues with our bodies." Using these periods of enhanced awareness of His tangible presence, God has etched in our

---

[24] Charles Finney, *Charles G. Finney: An Autobiography*, (Old Tappan, N.J.: Fleming H. Revell Company, 1876, renewed 1908), 20-21.

minds the concept written of in Psalm 84 by the Sons of Korah. "My soul yearns, even faints, for the courts of the Lord; my heart and my flesh cry out for the living God" (Psalm 84:2). As our flesh has cried out for the living God He has repeatedly answered with awesome displays of His love and power. Each experience with God has been followed by a period of profound supernatural peace.

There have been other times when the weighty presence of God has come on both of us simultaneously as one flesh while worshiping together in a church or conference setting. When this occurs it is certainly possible to resist the relaxed feeling in our bodies and continue to stand. We have found, however, that the intensity of our experiencing God's manifest presence increases if these sensations are welcomed and not refused. Again, God could choose to overpower us without our permission like He did to Paul on the road to Damascus, but the Holy Spirit loves to be welcomed and honored in our lives.

As the perception of God's supernatural touch grows, it becomes progressively more difficult to remain standing. Sitting down is a common first response, but it often reaches the point at which it is difficult to remain in any position other than lying down across chairs or on the floor. Although it can happen quickly at times resulting in a literal fall, with Linda and I it often occurs slowly and progressively. Often we both wind up in graceless horizontal positions as we yield our bodies to the presence and power of God's Spirit. We refer to this surprising and powerful interaction with the Holy Spirit as "melting." Just like a good chocolate bar left in the car on a hot, sunny day slowly melts, so our bodies responding to the presence of the Holy Spirit slowly melt.

This happened quite forcefully to us once during the evening worship time at a Christian conference. We stopped singing for a moment because we felt led to pray for one another. In a totally unplanned and unexpected way we both melted down into our chairs, ending the service awkwardly slumped against each other. Due to the overwhelming presence of God, we were hardly aware of our surroundings. We remained in that odd but pleasant state for an extended period of time. When we were finally willing and able to get up to leave, only a handful of people remained from the hundreds who had previously been there. This was a major encounter for the both of us with the tangible presence of God's Holy Spirit. It was one of the most powerful and memorable supernatural experiences of our lives!

Linda and I have learned that giving and receiving the presence and gifts of the Holy Spirit is meant to be a regular part of our everyday lives. Serious and significant interactions with God can and do occur in casual settings. The sharing together of spiritual experiences with a marital partner is a practical and non-threatening way to learn how to participate in the supernatural realm. The intimate relationship of marriage is the ideal setting for a man and woman to feel the intimacy of God's loving touch. The manifestations which occur are normal and natural to those who receive them. They are not intended to be used as a sideshow. These experiences are a valid portion of truly abundant life.

The frequency of these one flesh interactions with God as a couple is not always on a daily basis, yet it is not unusual for them to be part of our shared worship and prayer. We can choose to enter His presence in this tangible way almost at will. We can intentionally step into the divine glory of His manifest presence. His touch will be made available to those who keep asking, who keep seeking, and who keep knocking. The intensity and satisfaction of intimacy with God is surprising and amazing, actually surpassing what can be enjoyed from physical intimacy in marriage.

These have been overwhelming experiences of amazing oneness with each other and with God. We have had moments at which it seemed we became completely one with God in spirit, soul, and body. Our perception and understanding of communion with our supernatural God has been changed forever. We sense that we are just beginning to touch on the realms of union with God in the way Jesus described to the disciples – just as a branch is connected to the vine (John 15).

SUPERNATURAL CHANGE

Throughout my life I have known that my inner nature is that of a peacemaker. God placed this within me as I was formed within my mother's womb. Inside, this is who I truly am.

Yet, it has also been clear that there has been an angry disposition which has risen up within me innumerable times, and has been obvious to others on many occasions. This intense anger is a familial curse passed on to me by the kingdom of darkness through the generations which preceded me. I never asked for this – I received it as an unwelcome gift. However, without doubt I willingly participated with it many times, increasing its strength of grip in my life and its ill effects on those who have known me.

When I prayed with Jeff and Brandy Helton to receive deliverance and inner healing, we prayed specifically against the spirit of anger and commanded it to leave. Immediately I felt much more at peace with who I was and became considerably more kind and compassionate to those around me. In the ensuing months, the extreme anger that had plagued me for years only arose one more time. Even at that time, the uncontrollable feelings within me were much weaker and shorter lived than so many times in the past.

Following our supernatural experiences at the *Texas Ablaze* conference in Dallas, the depth and consistency of my inner peace has been greatly strengthened. From time to time I still feel a much smaller degree of anger attempting to build up inside me. Now, however, I immediately recognize the feeling of rage within my spirit and soul, and as soon as it is identified, the fury is defeated by God's presence that dwells within me. The anger leaves and is replaced immediately by a very pleasing sense of inner calm and peace, which I know only comes through the presence of the Holy Spirit.

My countenance and manner of relating with Linda and other people have profoundly changed since being touched by God's presence in such an astounding way. This was not accomplished by behavioral modification or concerted effort on my part. I had tried to defeat my anger using self-control, but had miserably failed. This change was supernaturally achieved through the replacement of the spirit of anger by the Prince of Peace. The extreme anger, which had tormented me and many others around me for years, was miraculously gone! And three years later it has not returned. The One who is in me "is greater than the one who is in the world" (1 John 4:4).

Supernatural Healing

Another effect of dwelling in the supernatural is that healing often occurs by the Spirit of God. Last year, while snorkeling in the Indian Ocean at low tide, Linda sustained a severe abrasion on her left shin from scraping against a coral formation. The injury bled for hours and left her in a great deal of pain. By the end of the second day it was showing signs of infection. Several of us surrounded Linda, proclaiming God's desire and miraculous ability to heal diseases of the skin (2 Kings 5:14; Matthew 8:3, 10:8). A Kenyan sister named Nellie, who had a gift for healing, laid her hand on the oozing wounds and prayed that God would stop the infection. Although we had no access to appropriate antibiotics, the infection subsided overnight. By the next morning Linda's leg looked remarkably better! Supernatural healing had occurred in her body by the power of God!

With the infection gone we were able to enjoy the remainder of our trip. However, during the long flight home we noticed a lump developing beneath the skin, near the bone of Linda's lower leg. We again prayed for healing, but the bulge increased gradually in size and the pain in the area intensified.

The morning after returning home we had the leg examined by a local orthopedic surgeon. He lanced the lesion, a deep cyst from the periostium of the tibia bone. We packed the opening twice a day with sterile gauze, while the cultures showed no sign of infection, but the cyst continued to exude a steady flow of clear yellow fluid. Twice a week we returned to the physician and with each visit, he advised us that surgery was the only way to be sure the oozing would stop.

Along with several strong brothers and sisters in Christ, we continued daily asking God to supernaturally heal this non-healing wound. Yet, after more than a month of daily packing, the constant dripping of fluid continued unabated. The three-year-old daughter of a friend looked quizzically at Linda and asked, "Why is your leg crying?"

Early one Sunday morning Linda and I were worshiping together in the church sanctuary, hours before the first service was scheduled to begin. As I prayed yet again for God to miraculously heal her injury, Linda received the revelation that a demonic spirit had entered her leg and was literally mocking the power, glory, and healing ability of *Jehovah Rapha* – the Lord our Healer (Exodus 15:26).

While praying in tongues, the Holy Spirit came upon me. With greater confidence and authority than I had ever before experienced, I laid my hand on Linda's injured leg and commanded the mocking spirit to leave. With strength and boldness that rose up from within my spirit, I prayed over Linda with more power and fervency than ever before. She immediately felt a physical release as the demonic spirit left her body. We both knew something remarkable and divine had occurred in that moment.

Minutes later we removed the bandage from Linda's lower leg. When we had earlier dressed the wound it still leaked continually. Now the dripping had completely ceased, never to return. Jesus healed Linda's injury that day, miraculously demonstrating His power over the enemy and over sickness. It was an astounding and joyful experience to share together, as one flesh, this awesome encounter with our true and living God.

SUPERNATURAL SELF-CONTROL

The day before I submitted the first chapter of this manuscript to our publisher, Linda and I experienced an intense attack from darkness. Although we both sensed this in the realm of the spirit, the assault on Linda was particularly severe. While on a long walk that night we hardly said a word. A lying spirit (1 Kings 22:22) put many thoughts in Linda's mind. The Spirit of wisdom (Isaiah 11:2) advised her that many of these thoughts need not be spoken. Self-control, part of the fruit of the Spirit Linda had received, enabled her to remain silent for a long twenty minutes as we walked. Meanwhile, I was totally confused.

Linda and I long to take these walks together on a regular basis. They are precious times we look forward to, when we can converse without interruption. Yet, this night my wife obviously wasn't talking at all. It made no sense to my natural mind. However, in the supernatural realm God allowed me to recognize we were both being attacked by a spiritual force outside of ourselves. He filled me with the gifts of patience and self-control. Without them I would have overreacted with an emotional response that would have made the situation much worse.

Because we had a supernatural marriage, we were both empowered to pass through the struggles of the evening with spiritual understanding of the situation and confidence that the attack would soon be defeated. Jesus was faithful and triumphant that night. Paul said that due to the presence and power of the Spirit of God, "We are hard pressed on every side, but not crushed; perplexed, but not in despair; persecuted, but not abandoned; struck down, but not destroyed" (2 Corinthians 4:8-9).

By the next day our peace was restored and this manuscript was successfully sent in to the publisher. Without the Spirit of God within us, lacking His presence in the center of our marriage, the result would have been far different. God had supernaturally prepared us to identify, resist, and ultimately defeat a vicious attack from the kingdom of darkness.

SUPERNATURAL OPPORTUNITY

During a recent visit to China, Linda and I were invited to have dinner with a communist leader in Beijing. Chairman W[25] began the visit by greeting us in a formal meeting room. As I sat at Chairman W's right hand in a large, ornate, and very uncomfortable chair, we sipped tea together while stiffly discussing current events in China.

After thirty minutes of talking through a translator about nothing of real importance, we drove across town to a private

---

[25] Due to safety's sake, I must withhold his full name here. Chairman W will also be referred to as the chairman through the rest of this section.

government restaurant and health spa. Inside the imposing facility were several dining rooms, each exquisitely decorated with walls covered in gold leaf, beautiful Chinese artwork, magnificent hardwood tables and tastefully upholstered chairs. The entire building was immaculate and pristine, artfully designed, and skillfully fabricated.

As dinner was prepared, we visited more with the chairman and a few other subordinate leaders in a receiving area adjacent to the table in our private dining room. Each of us began to relax. The conversation became more casual, focusing on jobs, families, and areas of personal interest.

When we sat down to eat, Linda pulled out a bright yellow set of plastic chopsticks that were attached at one end by the head of a smiling duck. They were meant for small children, but Linda had brought them as a joke to lighten the mood of our time with the Chinese leaders. They laughed as we also laughed along with them – the mood of the meeting completely changing through this one disarmingly silly act. The twelve courses of food presented to us that day were the most amazing we have ever seen. What was more amazing, however, was the change in the direction of our conversation for the remainder of the meal.

For the next two hours, the chairman asked us a series of questions about what it is like to be a Christian in America. He inquired about the definition of terms such as church, pastor, elder, and deacon. He wanted to know what worship meant and invited us to describe a typical week of church activity. The chairman seemed concerned that allegiance to God might keep Christians from patriotically serving their country.

He asked me what the most important thing in my life was and I told him, "God is number one." When he inquired what would be next I immediately responded with, "Linda is number two." As he laughed, the chairman then questioned Linda, "What do you think about being number two?" She confidently replied, "I love it! In fact, God is also number one to me. Dan is very pleased to be number two after God."

The mouth and the eyes of the chairman opened widely. Coming from a society where the communist government is supreme and men dominate their families, it was shocking for him to hear Linda publicly say, "Dan is number two." Even more surprising to him was the fact that I accepted and even encouraged her to consider me to be in such a position under the supremacy of God in her life. We went on to explain more about how men and women relate to each other in Christian marriage with mutual respect, resulting in both being the recipients of love and honor. We shared with the chairman how this type of marital relationship is beneficial for any society.

This was a delightful and unique opportunity to discuss the treasure of abundant life in God with a powerful communist leader. It was given to us as a gift, divinely ordained and supernaturally accomplished through weak vessels much like jars of clay. Paul said ordinary people, like us, diffuse the glory of God through their lives and words: "But we have this treasure in jars of clay to show that this all-surpassing power is from God and not from us" (2 Corinthians 4:7). Through connectedness with the Holy Spirit, our relationship with God was maturing. Like Jesus, we were growing "in favor with God and men" (Luke 2:52).

The next morning we left the gilded halls of the wealthy and moved on to minister to those whose lives were of the opposite extreme. Traveling to the countryside, we spent the day with an underground church, which literally met underground in the shelter of a large cave. In the natural realm they seemed very poor, yet the Spirit of the Lord was upon them and they enjoyed riches that cannot be measured in either U.S. dollars or Chinese yuan.

During worship in a cave, Linda and I noticed a middle-aged married woman whose face shone like that of an angel. She maintained a countenance of peace which belied the challenges of her life. She turned out to be the pastor of that particular underground church. In spite of the hardships faced in life, she had everything she needed for life and godliness (2 Peter 1:3). The opportunity we were given to meet and pray with this precious sister was no less significant than witnessing to Chairman W the day before.

The woman's face and life radiated the glory of God for all to see. Neither her poverty nor the oppressive system of government in which she lived could keep the Light of the world from emitting out of every part of her being. It is the intense desire of my heart to see that same glory shining out of me, my marriage, and all who pursue intimacy with God.

Transition into Supernatural Marriage

In Ruth Ward Heflin's book, *River Glory*, she writes, "God's desire is to take us places we can't ask to be taken because we don't know they even exist. He wants to give us experiences that we could never request because we have never yet even dreamed of them."[26] This is the essence of transitioning to supernatural marriage. Linda and I did not know what to ask for when we cried out to God at the time of our twenty-fifth anniversary. But the Spirit of God interceded for us with groans that words could not express. Paul writes there will be things our spirits are crying out for which we're not even asking for with words. He writes: "But if we hope for what we do not yet have, we wait for it patiently. In

[26]Ruth Ward Heflin, *River Glory*, (Hagerstown, MD: McDougal Publishing, 1999), 56.

the same way, the Spirit helps us in our weakness. We do not know what we ought to pray for, but the Spirit himself intercedes for us with groans that words cannot express" (Romans 8:25-26). God answered our passionate prayers with clarity and glorious simplicity. Once experienced, the revelation of supernatural marriage is not complicated at all. In fact, it is amazingly simple and simply amazing.

As we continue to pursue increased intimacy with God through communing with the Holy Spirit, it is important to realize that the timing of His response is not within our control. Fortunately, God is completely wise and knows the perfect timing for all things. Temporal urgency within us is a sign of passionate desire for what we seek. Although passion for God is a laudable trait, we must remember that God is completely sovereign over all that occurs in His Kingdom. Because of God's love and faithfulness, we maintain implicit trust in the absolute goodness of His plan. As we hope for what we do not yet have, unswerving faith enables us to wait for it patiently (Romans 8:25).

Undoubtedly, the fact that you are reading this book is evidence that you are being drawn more and more into the supernatural realm of God. You have been summoned by name. You are His and He knows you by name: "I have summoned you by name; you are mine," God says (Isaiah 43:1). You are specifically chosen by God, having been predestined to experience all that has been planned for you. He will work out everything that is required to achieve the purpose of His will in your life: "In him we were also chosen, having been predestined according to the plan of him who works out everything in conformity with the purpose of his will" (Ephesians 1:11).

The order and intention of each event in your spiritual formation has been ordained by the Spirit of God so that His will would be done in your earthly life just as it is in heaven (Matthew 6:10). This will be accomplished only if you remain supernaturally connected with the One whose will we desire to follow. May you and your spouse participate fully in the glorious Kingdom of God as you join Him in the supernatural realm.

Chapter Thirteen

SUPERNATURAL ROMANCE: EMOTIONAL INTIMACY

THE PERFECT MARRIAGE

God is unquestionably an extreme romantic. Soon after speaking life into Adam, God expressed awareness of man's need for emotional and physical intimacy with another created being of equal stature. God said, "It is not good for the man to be alone" (Genesis 2:18). Through forming Eve from Adam's rib, our Father produced the essential second half of the first marital relationship. These two individuals, now united as one, became the original prototype for all human romance and marriages for ages to come.

The setting for this love relationship was idyllic – a man and a woman in an eternally perfect physical environment, supernaturally made complete by the manifest presence of God. It is said that God came down and walked among them in the cool of the day. No one since that time has had the same type of relationship with the Father, save Jesus Himself. It was a time where there was no sin to separate them from God. They walked in complete righteousness before Him and did not have any sense of shame, guilt, or inferiority in God's presence. They felt at home in God's presence because that was what they were created for. They were also naked "and they felt no shame" (Genesis 2:25), totally familiar with each other and intimately connected to the One who consistently provided everything that was required.

Adam and Eve were the first couple to experience the extreme bliss of supernatural marriage. They had the perfect marriage in the perfect place. Their oneness with each other and with God was lost through rejection of His lordship. Yet, their relationship prior to the fall stands as an example to all who seek to fulfill the ultimate plan of God for holy matrimony.

The intense intimacy in God's plan for marriage is celebrated through the romantic allusions in the Song of Solomon in the Old Testament, reiterated by the apostle Paul in his New Testament letters, and demonstrated by Jesus' passionate return to claim His bride in John's revelatory visions.

POWERFUL ATTRACTION THROUGH PASSION

In Psalm 42 the Sons of Korah write of an almost insatiable desire for God and a willingness to go anywhere to meet with Him. Their desire for God is expressed like this: "As the deer pants for streams of water, so my soul pants for you, O God. My soul thirsts for God, for the living God. When can I go and meet with God?" (Psalm 42:1-2) This Scripture is reminiscent of the powerful attraction experienced between husband and wife, the passion which sometimes demands that they escape to a place of privacy where they can reunite as one flesh. Healthy sexual attraction between partners in marriage mirrors the strong desire God wishes us to have in our relationship with Him. After completing creation on the sixth day, God transitioned into His Sabbath rest knowing that "it was very good" (Genesis 1:31). Part of this creation was the physical attraction in man for woman, and later in woman for man. We can say with confidence that God placed this powerful desire in each of us, and it is also very good.

Romantic, even sexual, symbolism is used regularly in the Song of Solomon. We belong to our Lover and His "desire is for me" (Song of Solomon 7:10). Through this beautiful allegorical story, the wisest of earthly kings prophetically points to the extreme intimacy that Jesus as the Bridegroom expects when He is ultimately united with the church as His perfect bride. The One who gave us ardent physical desire for each other in marriage is the same God who wants us involved in a passionate love relationship with Him.

GIVING OURSELVES TO GOD AND OUR SPOUSE

God's desire is that we willingly submit every aspect of who we are to Him, the perfect Lover of our souls. In marriage we symbolically act out this submission to Him every time we surrender our hearts, our wills, or our bodies to each other. In supernatural marriage this yielding to our partner's needs and desires occurs on a regular basis. It is led by the Spirit of Christ and is done out of reverence for Him. This is one reason why Paul, in the context of marriage, wrote, "Submit to one another out of reverence for Christ" (Ephesians 5:21).

If Jesus' lordship is to be complete, it is necessary that each of us fully submit our body to Him. This is taught regularly to young men and women during courtship years, in the hope they would remain pure in their physical relationships. However, lordship of our bodies is no less important after marriage is established than before. During every part of life your body is meant for the Lord

(1 Corinthians 6:13). When we have ears to hear what the Spirit speaks and consistently obey what we have heard, we will do the things with our physical bodies that most honor and glorify God. He will lead us into the very best ways to bless our marital partners through submission to their needs during sexual intimacy.

How do you honor God with your body in marriage? Your body is not your own. It belongs to God. Paul wrote to the Corinthians in his first letter: "Do you not know that your body is a temple of the Holy Spirit, who is in you, whom you have received from God? You are not your own; you were bought at a price. Therefore honor God with your body" (1 Corinthians 6:19-20). Not only does your body belong to God, but also He has given it to your spouse. In fact, Paul goes on to talk about this not too much later in the same letter, giving some wisdom about marriage. He said:

> The husband should fulfill his marital duty to his wife, and likewise the wife to her husband. The wife's body does not belong to her alone but also to her husband. In the same way, the husband's body does not belong to him alone but also to his wife. Do not deprive each other except by mutual consent and for a time, so that you may devote yourselves to prayer.   – 1 Corinthians 7:3-6

God uses your body as a powerful tool through which both His and your love can be beautifully demonstrated to your partner. In truth, even the love you think is yours originated within the heart of God. In supernatural marriage His perfect love flows through each partner to the other, without restriction or pause. The pure and holy love of the Father is the eternally flowing wellspring of life, the ultimate source of everything needed to establish and maintain spiritual, emotional, and physical oneness in marriage. And one aspect of the way love is shown is through sexual intimacy. But before we get into sexual intimacy, it will be important to first discuss the need for emotional intimacy. Before a spouse ever feels connected in a sexual way, there is a great need to connect on an emotional, romantic level.

Everyday Romance

The most important romantic events leading to successful sexual relations are those which occur hours, days, or even years earlier. These are the things that establish a strong bond between the marriage partners and a closer connection with each other. These are essential in maintaining long-term emotional intimacy.

A marriage which exhibits reliable and enjoyable everyday romance is well equipped to proceed smoothly into sexual intimacy. A marital relationship based on sexuality, however, is ill-prepared for the establishing of a loving, trusting, and long-term relationship. This is one reason why God wisely commands us to abstain from sex prior to marriage. Although all aspects of sexuality become freely available to spouses in marriage, the less physical, even non-sexual forms of romantic relatedness continue to be of extreme importance.

The key to effective everyday romance is for each partner to honestly and consistently express love to the other in ways that can be recognized and received. The love communicated must be both selfless (*agape*) and lifelong (*phileo*).[27] It is entirely appropriate that daily expressions of love might encourage a spouse toward sexual intimacy. However, the primary purpose of regular romantic gestures is to convey love, acceptance, and genuine interest in fulfilling the needs of your spouse. It must not be intended or perceived as manipulation of any kind. Manipulation is dangerous, and even deadly to romantic relationships.

---

[27] See Chapter 10, "Styles of Marriage: Exemplary Marriage" for a more complete definition of what I am referring to here.

It is critically important that both partners know how they and their spouse are most comfortable communicating love. In his book, *The Five Love Languages,*[28] Gary Chapman describes the five primary ways in which men and women express their love within close relationships. He describes these as words of affirmation, quality time, receiving gifts, acts of service, and physical touch. Most of us can appreciate all five love languages to a degree, but are particularly moved by one in particular. I want to encourage you to read Gary Chapman's book and have fun yet serious conversations with your marital partner as to which love languages each of you enjoys the most, and which are more difficult to relate to.

In romantic gestures to your spouse, it is often wise to use the language they most naturally receive, but do not limit yourself to only this. Share with your spouse which love language is your favorite and help them learn to speak your love language. Your marital relationship is further enriched by stretching each other toward becoming facile at giving and receiving love through all five of the languages.

Linda and I have made great efforts toward becoming multilingual in the communication of love. We try to use all the love languages effectively and regularly. We don't just choose the one that comes most naturally to us, but we work on the ones we know will touch the heart of the other person on the deepest level. We all have a tendency to think that the way our spouses want to receive love would be the same as the way we want to receive it. Many times your spouse will want to receive love in a different way than you are used to giving it. You have to speak their primary love language for them to best understand it.

---

[28]Gary Chapman, *The Five Love Languages,* (Northfield Publishing: Chicago, 1992).

The main purpose of expressing heartfelt emotional interest to your lover is that the two of you would become united more and more as one. It is extremely enjoyable and unifying to express thoughts to your spouse such as,

"I like you."

"I enjoy you."

"I care for you."

"I appreciate you."

"I desire to be with you."

"I love you."

And, "You are very special to me."

These can be conveyed through any of the love languages. Regardless of the means, the communication of these thoughts transmits the messages of love and tenderness, which are crucial to both emotional and physical intimacy in marriage.

It is vitally important to be affectionate and flirty with your spouse on a regular basis, not only when physical sexual relations are desired. There is great enjoyment and pleasure in romantically expressing love and tenderness without immediate plans to progress further in making love. It is particularly good for the husband to plan ahead of time that his advances will not physically go beyond a certain point that hour, or perhaps that day. This intentional delay of gratification communicates to his wife that expressing pure love to her is his ultimate goal, not having sex. Physical and verbal demonstrations of affection are meant to be much more than a planned series of actions focused on achieving sexual pleasure. There is enormous value in every step taken along the way.

PRACTICAL TIPS FOR EMOTIONAL ROMANCE

Allow me to share with you a few random things Linda and I have found to be fun and helpful in establishing and maintaining our everyday romance:

- Be physically near each other as much as is practical.

- Speak honest, complimentary words about your spouse to others. Do this both with and without them being present.

- God loves it when you have a thankful heart, and your spouse will, too! Express thanks often concerning both big and little things.

- When separated in a crowd, periodically acknowledge each other's presence using eye contact and a smile, brief verbal communication, or even a hint of a kiss passed through the air with no physical contact. We actually learned this years ago from our pet parakeet who blew us kisses from across the room.

- Briefly touch as you pass one another, whether alone, in a group, or swimming in the YMCA pool.

- Make very short phone calls to each other while at work, just long enough to say, "I love you," or "I miss you massively."

- Loving or flirty text messages can be extremely fun as well. Be bold, but be wise.

- Write capital letters on each other's hands or backs with your fingers, which symbolize tender thoughts. (We use ILYVVVM! to say, "I love you very, very, very much!")

- Send words of love and affirmation to each other in creative e-mails.

- Write love notes on napkins placed within sack lunches taken to work. It is amazing what can be effectively communicated to a spouse through these words, discretely kept from the eyes of co-workers.

- Mail "Thank You" or "I Love You" cards to each other to be delivered at home or at work.

- Send flowers or bring home small gifts for no particular reason other than to communicate how special your spouse is to you.

- When possible, play music in the car or at home that you both enjoy. It is particularly valuable to listen together to music that has inspired both of you into greater intimacy with God.

- Play romantic games together. For example, have code words that can be spoken in public places with which you can easily communicate private and intimate thoughts to one another.

- Reminisce regularly about past fun and romantic experiences together.

- Plan a trip for your spouse to a surprise destination celebrating a big birthday or other special event. The extravagance of the trip is not important. The key is demonstrating love in the planning and forethought. Design the trip to include ample couple time.

- Flirt frequently. Be creative. It's fun!

- Holding hands is really nice, also. You can do it almost anywhere without restriction or embarrassment. We did a lot of this on our first date and have continued to enjoy it frequently ever since.

- Sensuously share a large chocolate truffle.

- Exercise with each other regularly, even if it is only walking a mile together while talking.

- Eat as many meals together as possible. It is very helpful to leave the television off. Visit about significant events of the day and try to listen at least as much as you talk.

- Establish a bedtime routine and follow it whenever able. Linda and I enjoy cuddling together on the sofa each night while we read Scripture to one another. Then we pray together for whatever length of time seems right that night before falling asleep.

- Finally, each night, through words and touch, express love to each other one last time before going to sleep. Being reminded that you are one with each other and one with God, you will rest peacefully through each night.

WHY NOT BE NICE?

For years Linda and I have had an expression one of us will say to the other when thanked for being exceptionally sweet. We commonly respond with a basic axiom of how we treat one another, "Why *not* be nice?" At the moment it is said mostly in fun, but being nice is a seriously important concept in the everyday romance of marriage.

Kindness and gentleness are critical in maintaining the romantic ambiance of a long-term close relationship. When there is a divergence of opinion between spouses on a particular issue, it is possible and remarkably effective to retain the fruit of the Spirit in dealing with the situation. Nothing of value is ever gained by winning a battle with your mate. Even in moments of intense frustration and confusion it is completely possible to be gentle and kind.

When strong words need to be spoken, they can be enveloped in *agape* love. There is no viable reason to not be nice to your life partner.

THE GOLDEN RULE

Knowing how to endearingly relate to a partner in marriage is truly not difficult. Jesus condensed the message of all known Scripture into one phrase we refer to as "the Golden Rule." Jesus said, "So in everything, *do to others what you would have them do to you*, for this sums up the Law and the Prophets" (Matthew 7:12, emphasis mine) His seemingly simple instruction is beautifully applicable to all forms of interpersonal association, particularly the intimate relational connectedness within the marriage covenant. When we treat our lover the way we would honestly love to be treated, the emotional and romantic environment of our marriage will undoubtedly improve.

If one partner in marital union consistently fulfills the legitimate desires and needs of the other in their daily life together, it is much more likely that his or her wishes will ultimately be realized. It is a general rule that gentleness shown leads to gentleness received. This is true in most relationships, but is most reliably valid when one's spouse actively seeks to honor God.

Kindness extended for the purpose of manipulation or control is very detrimental to a relationship and should be completely avoided. However, nothing is more romantic than persistently pursuing and doing the things that most deeply bless the one you love. If you have ears to hear what the Spirit says (Revelation 3:22), there is no question God will supernaturally lead you to know where, when, and how to best show love to your partner in marriage. So, with encouragement of romance as my primary goal, I ask you, "Why *not* be nice?" Try it. I promise there will be blessing as a result.

Chapter Fourteen

SUPERNATURAL ROMANCE: SEXUAL INTIMACY

ow that we have seen the importance of emotional intimacy in the marriage relationship, we turn our attention to the issue of sexual intimacy. In this chapter I want to deal with how God created our sexuality and then give some tips on how to pursue your spouse and enjoy sexual intimacy in the context of supernatural marriage. As we surrender our bodies and sexuality to the lordship of Christ, God will teach us eternal principles that will forever change our lives.

THE SIMPLICITY OF SEXUALITY

On one hand, God created human sexuality to be amazingly simple. The essential aspects of how we mate to reproduce our-selves can be taught in a short period of time. The sexual drive, which is also known as libido, placed within us makes it possible for most to succeed in the basic act of sexual intercourse with little or no rehearsal. Scientists have analyzed the anatomy, physiology, and emotional responses involved in sexual relations to the point at which it seems they could be completely understood by anyone and carried off perfectly by all who are willing to put forth the effort to learn.

On the other hand it is apparent that, from the frequent misunderstanding, unhealthy application, and overall confusion surrounding sexuality, this area of human interaction is also extremely complex. Poets have written innumerable lines of verse, while fiction writers have produced countless romantic novels. The wisest researchers admit there is still much we do not know when it comes to human sexuality. As we try to explain this transcendent interaction between two individuals' bodies, souls, and spirits connecting together, it becomes increasingly obvious that this multifaceted creation of God is not simple at all.

Proverbs 30 refers to sexual intimacy as something which cannot really be understood. Agur wrote: "There are three things that are too amazing for me, four that I do not understand: the way of an eagle in the sky, the way of a snake on a rock, the way of a ship on the high seas, and the way of a man with a maiden" (Proverbs 30:18-19). In agreement with Agur, I would say that sex, enjoyed within the covenant of marriage, is simply "amazing."

As with other aspects of the relationship between spouses in supernatural marriage, it is important to not settle for mediocrity in lovemaking. Sexual play is created to be enjoyable and satisfying, with no sense of shame or guilt. At times it can be absolutely astonishing. Do not accept *pretty good* as the ultimate goal for sexual intimacy in your marital union. Every spouse can and should put continual effort into optimizing this very pleasurable aspect of marriage. God places no limit on the bliss that can be experienced together in physical intimacy with your spouse. It is appropriate and good that we should spend a lifetime together with our mate pursuing the very best ways to enjoy this precious gift from our loving Father.

Afraid to Talk About Sexuality

Perhaps the most intimidating section to write in this entire book has been this one on sexual intimacy. I have always considered sexuality to be the most personal of subjects. It is not something I regularly talk about with friends or with strangers. Sex is rarely mentioned in sermons, Sunday school classes, or during informal conversations between believers. When sexual relations are discussed in Christian circles, it is usually in the negative context of problems caused by physical intimacy outside of marriage.

I began collecting my thoughts concerning sexuality recently while on a plane flying to Saint Maarten to work on this book. As I typed the title, "Sexual Intimacy" at the top of the page, I immediately felt a bit uncomfortable because the stranger next to me could easily see the screen of my laptop. Using creative liberty I quickly erased what had been entered and changed it to the words Linda and I use when we want to talk about sex in public places. Instead of using the "S" word, we simply smile and say, "you know!" For several weeks we have laughingly referred to this as the "you know" chapter.

Sex is frequently brought to our attention in dishonorable and perverse ways by the powers of darkness through mass media. Television, movies, magazines, and the Internet encourage us to become obsessed with sexual relations, because doing so increases the dividends received by their stockholders. Human sexuality is pushed upon all of us in its vilest and most abusive extremes by the powers of darkness.

There are certainly many settings in which the frank discussion of sex is inappropriate; however, most Christians are unnecessarily uncomfortable talking about this subject due to misunderstanding it, inhibition concerning it, and lack of appreciation of its beauty and value in our lives. Sexuality is a vitally important subject for believers to talk about before, during, and even after marriage.

On top of all that, our church culture has generally adopted a secular view of sexuality, other than encouraging celibacy outside of marriage. It is seen as a private part of home life which is not directly related to other parts of life such as work or even religion, for that matter. This view is not only incorrect, but also very dangerous to the body of Christ. It is an attempt by the kingdom of darkness to hide and ultimately destroy this gloriously wonderful gift from God. Of all the people in the world, we should have a correct understanding and application of our sexuality, because we are intimate with the very One who created us and originally intended marriage for His good pleasure.

God desires to be intimately involved with every aspect of our lives. In the Old Testament He tells Joshua, "As I was with Moses, so I will be with you; I will never leave you nor forsake you" (Joshua 1:5). The gospel of Matthew ends with Jesus encouraging His disciples with the words, "And surely I am with you always, to the very end of the age" (Matthew 28:20). Does God withdraw His holy presence from us during the times we are passionately involved in sexual relations within the covenant of marriage? The answer to this is no, He does not. He is there in our midst. Our supernatural connectedness with God is no less real during sexual intercourse than at any other point in our lives.

Paul instructs us that we are told to "pray continually" (1 Thessalonians 5:17). Communion is not just something we take on Sunday with bread and wine or, for others, crackers and grape juice. We are called to commune with God every moment of our lives. Our intimate connectedness with God continues, and is even enhanced, through pure and undefiled sexual intimacy. The periodically repeated physical oneness of husband and wife allegorically reminds us of the supernatural oneness God is establishing between the church and Himself. This beautiful analogy, expressed frequently throughout the Bible, is extremely important in the Kingdom of God. It is a wondrous thing to be consciously aware of God's glorious presence at all times in life – before, during, and after intimate marital relations.

Jesus ultimately requires that He be Lord of all. This includes your body as well as your soul and your spirit. It truly honors God when you properly apply and fully enjoy the sexual desires and abilities created within you and your spouse. The physical experience of oneness in marriage can be incredibly poignant and exhilarating. It helps establish and maintain a lifetime bond between marital partners and reminds us of the passionate intimacy Jesus will finally enjoy with us when we become His perfect bride.

Eternal Principles through Sexual Intimacy

Most people recognize the significant role sexual intimacy plays in the interpersonal relationships of husbands and wives. Few of us, however, realize that sexuality can be used by God to teach us eternal principles and transform us into who He desires us to be. I learned this through an experience within my own marriage.

During our first twenty-four years together, Linda and I had been blessed with a wonderful marital relationship. Over time we learned how to respond well to each other's sexual needs and patterns. We were very satisfied with the ways we physically related to one another, until Linda went through deliverance prayer. At that moment in time everything changed.

Linda had always been wonderfully affectionate. For years I told her that she was the finest lover on earth. After her deliverance she was suddenly different and, as my son's high school T-shirt used to say, "Different is good!" Surprisingly, Linda was kinder, more loving, and even more joyful. Immediately we both began to enjoy our sexual intimacy even more than before. I was surprised, confused, astonished, and totally thrilled by the change that had taken place.

The increased presence of God's Spirit within Linda had literally changed who she was. The Holy Spirit in her supernaturally improved every aspect of how she and I related to one another, including our sexual relations. What was very good became even better. It was a modern day incarnation of Isaiah's prophecy that an already fertile field would explode in growth to become like a forest, "till the Spirit is poured upon us from on high, and the desert becomes a fertile field, and the fertile field seems like a forest" (Isaiah 32:15). The growth in Linda was amazing to behold.

I loved the way God had changed my wife. Linda's increased ability to selflessly give herself to me was an observable, experiential manifestation of God's supernatural presence within her. After months it became obvious to me that her transformation was not only real, but also permanent. Her enhanced ability to love led me, a few months later, to also learn how to receive and share the flowing river of God's love in my own life. Not surprisingly, when I enjoyed supernatural freedom I, too, became a more consistent and effective lover of my wife. There is no better stimulus for marital oneness and satisfaction than the shared presence of God, whose very essence is love.

Our experience of an increasingly gratifying relationship is meant to bless more than two. Many marital partners get stuck in the hopeless rut of waiting for their spouses to be more lovable before they are willing to be better lovers for their spouses. There is no justification for this attitude in a believer who trusts in the transforming love of God. Waiting to love well until a partner changes can easily grow into a life-long delay. Becoming a truly great lover can be the first step in the transformation of one's spouse. Even a desert can become a fertile field through a marriage partner filled with the glorious presence of God's Spirit (Isaiah 32:15).

SURRENDERED SEXUALITY

God's design and full intention is to use every aspect of who you are to build His eternal Kingdom. There are many classes taught and sermons delivered describing how we are to release our spirits, minds, jobs, families, possessions, and finances to God's control. What needs further emphasis in the church is that every portion of our sexuality, which is a direct gift from God, should also be fully surrendered to His control.

As mentioned previously, your body is not your own (1 Corinthians 6:19). It is a purchased possession of God which is shared by both you and your spouse. Your partner should have access to your physical body for purposes they are aware of, but also to fulfill needs that may not yet be recognized. Part of your responsibility as half of a one flesh relationship is to supply what is needed to accomplish things neither of you can do on your own. Satisfying sexual intimacy is one of these things.

Particularly at the beginning of marriage, spouses often have very different opinions concerning what is desirable and truly enjoyable within the realm of sexual play. At times it is important to be able to say "no" to an activity that might be uncomfortable, unpleasant, or seem to be unwise. In these instances it is very helpful if the "no" can be spoken in a kind way that leaves hope for the trying of other creative ideas in the future.

When resistance to any sexual activity is perceived to be coming from your partner, it is vital that it be stopped or delayed until receptivity is established. Consider a small child being encouraged to jump from a diving board to his father patiently waiting in the deep water below. It could emotionally injure the child to be pushed off the end of the board. Eventually, the jump is voluntarily made, leading to a lifetime of enjoying a wonderful form of recreation. Similarly, each spouse should coax the other into discovering new ways to relax and have fun together, but should never push the other into any form of physical intimacy.

UNSELFISH LOVE

Sexual play within marriage has many purposes including procreation, expression of love, physical demonstration of oneness, mutually shared pleasure, emotional release, stress relief, as well as physical satisfaction. Every one of these purposes is optimized when your primary goal in sexual interaction is that your spouse fully enjoys everything that is done. This is completely consistent with Paul's command in Philippians 2. He wrote, "Do nothing out of selfish ambition or vain conceit, but in humility consider others better than yourselves. Each of you should look not only to your own interests, but also to the interests of others" (Philippians 2:3-4).

There is no more reliable path to mutual sexual contentment than two partners sharing the safe playground of marital intimacy, each focused on helping the other to fully enjoy their shared oneness. The results are best when the goal of each lover is the same – the complete joy and satisfaction of their spouse. Shared selflessness is the key to both personal and collective fulfillment from sexual intimacy.

One area of frequent dispute between spouses is the frequency of their sexual interaction. After an orgasm it is typical for a man's libido to markedly decrease and then slowly build again over the next three to five days. This pattern is so common and predictable that it has led to the establishment of marital laws. For example, in March of 2009, Afghanistan passed a law allowing husbands to demand sex with their wives every four days.[29] The fact that such a law would even be considered clearly shows that the timing of peak interest in sex is often quite different in men and women.

The sequencing of decreasing and increasing libido in women is generally less predictable than in men. It tends to follow a more complex pattern which is often related to the monthly menstrual cycle. It can be very difficult, particularly during the first years of marriage, for a husband or wife to understand the sexual desires and needs of their partner. It is extremely helpful for each to recognize that the other's pattern of sexual libido is given to them by God with wisdom and purpose. Although their patterns of desire may not always mesh well, they are what they are and should be dealt with through gentleness, patience, and love.

---

[29] San Angelo Standard Times, Thursday, April 16, 2009, Section C, page 1 (copied from Associated Press).

KABUL–Dozens of young women braved crowds of bearded men screaming "dogs!" Wednesday to protest an Afghan law that lets husbands demand sex from their wives. Some of the men picked up small stones and pelted the women.

The warring protests highlight the explosive nature of the women's rights debate in Afghanistan. Both sides are girding for battle over the legislation, which has sparked an international uproar since being quietly signed into law last month.

The law says a husband can demand sex with his wife every four days, unless she is ill or would be harmed by intercourse. It also regulates when and for what reasons a wife may leave her home without a male escort.

Though the law would apply only to the country's Shiites, who make up less than 20 percent of Afghanistan's 30 million people, many fear its passage marks a return to Taliban-style oppression of women.

Correct timing can make all the difference in a woman's ability to respond and fully enjoy sexual relations. Patience is one of the fruit of the Spirit that God creates in our hearts, and wisdom is given to us directly by God. When a man is patient and allows wisdom to tell him when and how to pursue intimacy with his wife, the results are beyond amazing. It is said in real estate the three most important things are location, location, and location. Aside from the presence of true *agape* love in a marriage, the three most critical factors in shared sexual satisfaction are timing, timing, and timing.

On a given day a man may be amorous while his wife is not. This means neither that his libido is inappropriately high, nor that hers is inadequate. Similarly, it is normal that on some days the woman might be more interested in intimacy than her husband. Some asymmetry in the sexual desires of marital partners is nearly always present. Working through this difference may seem at times to be an insurmountable challenge. In truth, God designed the sexual libidos of men and women with perfect wisdom and purpose. This dissimilarity presents marital partners with a tremendous opportunity to submit to one another's needs "out of reverence for Christ" (Ephesians 5:21).

The best way to resolve this common source of tension between male and female spouses is to allow the love of God to flow through us to our partners. To do this we must first receive His supernatural love before we are able to give it away, as it is impossible to give away something without first possessing it. Once God's passionate love is in us, the Holy Spirit will provide wisdom and understanding of the best ways to communicate this love to our partners. Love is only a portion of what is supernaturally given to spouses who intimately commune with the Spirit of God. There are many aspects to His fruit, all of which contribute to our ability to intimately connect with our marital partners.

The fruit of the Spirit is valuable in every aspect of relating to one another in marriage, yet there is no area where it is more obviously important than that of physical intimacy. When the attributes of "love, joy, peace, patience, kindness, goodness, faithfulness, gentleness and self-control" (Galatians 5:22-23) are regularly present in a husband or wife, their capacity to satisfy the sexual needs of their partner is exponentially increased. This listing of virtuous qualities is a perfect description of the ultimate Lover. Although it is best that both partners demonstrate these gifts, even the supernatural spouse of an unbeliever can use them to bring abundant blessing to sexual intimacy within the marriage.

Ideally, perfect love from the Father flows freely through both partners in supernatural marriage, allowing them to share the depth, richness, and beauty of a love that has no end. Faithfulness to one's spouse demonstrates lasting commitment and reliability, which sets the stage for a relationship anchored in trust. Spirit-led patience and self-control result in the best time and place being chosen for physical intimacy, while kindness and goodness create a completely enjoyable environment for lovemaking. Each spouse is eternally one with God. As they join together to be fully one with each other, their perception of joy and experience of inner peace is supernaturally enhanced.

WISDOM IN SEXUAL INTIMACY

Paul writes to the Romans, "I want you to be wise about what is good, and innocent about what is evil. The God of peace will soon crush Satan under your feet" (Romans 16:19-20). It is vitally important for us to be wise throughout life concerning the best ways to experience physical intimacy. Sexuality within marriage is something created by God and is meant to be very good. Through it we participate in the creation of new life, share memorable demonstrations of love for one another, and strengthen the marital union by freely giving and receiving intense pleasure and love. Knowing how to gratify the needs of our spouses assists God in crushing Satan underneath our feet. Being good at sex requires being competent at physically pleasing one's partner and it also demands purity of heart and acceptance of Christ's complete lordship over each of our lives. It is wise to be good at things that really matter.

Satisfying sexuality decreases the desire of both men and women to look outside of the marriage for gratification. Certainly it does not, in itself, result in faithfulness. However, without doubt sexual dissatisfaction is a powerful tool used by Satan in the destruction of marital harmony. The pursuit of excellence in lovemaking is an enjoyable and effective way of maintaining innocence and purity in marriage. On top of all this, God-given faithfulness is another source of strength empowering us to defeat Satan.

Although usually quite important, sexual relations are not the primary focus of the healthiest marriages. There are situations in which physical intimacy is impossible, yet the marital union remains strong. Still, for most couples the joint level of satisfaction with physical intimacy is a sensitive and important indicator for the well-being of their relationship as a whole. Both should be pleased that their sexual needs, at whatever their level might be, are adequately met, while at the same time each experiences great joy in knowing their partner is sexually content.

When significant dissatisfaction with physical intimacy develops in one or both spouses over an extended period of time, it often indicates that something is awry in the marital relationship. If this signal is ignored, or if the problem is not successfully identified and dealt with, sexual frustration and dysfunction can persist for years. Spouses committed to following the ways of God may remain faithful in their actions while being pure in their minds and imaginations. Yet, it is quite clear to both partners that something is amiss.

It is valuable for spouses to regularly communicate with one another concerning their level of sexual contentment. Decreasing fulfillment with any aspect of marriage is best discussed when first noticed. We are blessed when we find wisdom and gain understanding (Proverbs 3:13), both of which are supplied by God. Wisdom allows us to identify problems while understanding shows us how to deal with them. When the source of difficulty is discovered and healed, every part of the marital relationship benefits.

Satisfying sexuality provides remarkable strength and stability for marriage. It helps both partners to maintain purity, remain faithful to God, and keep their marriage vows. There are many keys to gratifying physical intimacy.

PRACTICAL SUGGESTIONS FOR SEXUAL INTIMACY

Following are a few ways of sexual thinking and behaving which would bless almost any marital relationship. As you read through these, let them spark imagination in you and consider how you can implement some of them in your marital relationship.

- Don't take lovemaking too seriously. Laugh and act silly. Fully enjoy your most intimate friend. This is play, not work!

- Go to bed together and wake up together as often as possible. Make this your normal and most desired routine.

- Buy nice underwear and use them.

- Pay attention to hygiene and physical cleanliness.

- Reminisce about particularly special sexual times together as you pursue the making of memories for the future.

- Coax your partner toward intimacy, but never push them.

- Visual flirting is fun, even in a crowd. Catch each other's eyes with a prolonged gaze that clearly communicates your thoughts.

- Touch each other frequently in non-sexual ways. Gradually ramp up the intimacy of the touches when a receptive response is noticed.

- Don't be in a hurry. Take your time and enjoy the process.

- Ask questions like, "Does this feel good?" or "What would feel even better?"

- Make it a point to follow instructions from your partner well.

- Avoid getting into ruts. Variety really is the spice of life. Use your God-given creativity to vary the time, location, and surrounding ambiance of sexual play.

- Don't hesitate to repeat something tried and true that works really well for both of you.

- Occasionally try new positions and new ways of pleasuring one another.

- Say "no" when necessary, but always with love and hope so the person is not turned off for creativity in future intimacy.

- Surprise your lover from time to time with something completely unexpected.

- Discover a new way to enjoy the great outdoors.

- Never fear being ridiculous. You might miss experiencing something that is really fun.

- It is all right to be shy, but be sure your wishes are made known. When you feel sexual desire, communicate this in a way you are confident your partner will understand. Do not allow your spouse to miss the opportunity to enjoy you.

- Sometimes it makes perfect sense *not* to be practical. Miss a little sleep or skip the meeting at school. It's okay to be late for work once a quarter.

Intimacy in marriage is created to be immensely enjoyable. In it we can receive the immediate rewards of shared love and intense pleasure. We can also receive a profoundly satisfying relief from the stresses of life. Intimacy is most successful when each partner is particularly focused on the desires, needs, and eventual satisfaction of the other.

The greatest lover is the one most consistently filled with both *phileo* (familial, permanent) love and true *agape* (selfless, giving) love for his or her spouse. The most satisfying lover is not the one filled with the most *eros* (erotic desire), but the one who intensely and consistently pursues the ultimate good of the partner who is loved. This can be done regardless of the status of the other partner's relationship with God. A man or woman filled with the supernatural love of God will become the best possible lover, even for an unbelieving spouse.

Three years ago I made the decision to purposefully concentrate on my wife's physical needs and desires above my own. There are days when her goals are much less sexual than mine. It is best to show my love to her in alternative ways on those days, speaking her primary love language of quality time, or using my first love language of touch in platonic ways rather than through provocative flirtation. Patience and self-control are part of the fruit of the Spirit. Both qualities are often undervalued in the pursuit of marital intimacy. God will supernaturally supply these virtues to those who are wise enough to ask for them. Not surprisingly, they have led Linda and me into better understanding of the best times, places, and ways to enjoy our sexual relationship.

THE GOLDEN RULE OF SEXUAL INTIMACY

The primary axiom of sexual intimacy is the same as that of everyday romance. Jesus again reminds us: "So in everything, do to others what you would have them do to you, for this sums up the Law and the Prophets" (Matthew 7:12). This encourages you who are married to focus on doing what would most please your spouse. This includes discovering the romantic environments, the timing, and the techniques which best satisfy your partner's sexual desires. Their perception of what seems to be romantic and enjoyable is far more important than your personal opinion. One spouse making a real attempt to satisfy the needs of the other will improve the sexual relationship of the couple. When both partners approach sexuality with this attitude, they are released to enjoy the full potential of their physical intimacy together. The pleasure of this kind of oneness is truly amazing.

If you would like to know what is most pleasing to your partner in marriage you should plainly ask them. Many times, however, it can be difficult for them to answer such a direct question. Often it is better to ask the Holy Spirit what to do in any given situation. God has given you ears to hear what the Spirit is saying to you about your marriage and the best way to pursue sexual intimacy.

All you have to do is ask and listen, and He will tell you exactly what you need to know.

Human sexuality is an expression of love designed by God to simultaneously bless both participants. It is a shared physical demonstration of emotional and spiritual connectedness which honors both marriage and the Creator of marriage. God is love and He is the greatest of all lovers. He created every part of your sexual anatomy and gave you the physical desire which drew you to your spouse.

God is also the ultimate Teacher, who is willing and able to instruct you in what to do to satisfy the partner with whom you are one. Simply ask and it will be given to you: "Until now you have not asked for anything in my name. Ask and you will receive, and your joy will be complete" (John 16:24).

Chapter Fifteen

THE IMPORTANCE OF SEXUAL PURITY

We have now come near the end of our study on the subject of supernatural marriage. We have talked about how we are able to walk in it and what benefits it will bring to us as we walk with God and with our spouse in the realm of the supernatural. This type of supernatural marriage can only be carried out as we walk with the God of the supernatural, who is Jesus Christ Himself. But before we conclude our study, I want to share about the importance of sexual purity in keeping marriage securely anchored in the realm of the supernatural. If we do not possess purity in our hearts and lives, we are opening up a door to the enemy and inviting him to come in to steal and kill and destroy (John 10:10).

God is powerful and majestic – full of righteousness and justice. He is feared by those who oppose Him because of His capability and willingness, when needed, to respond with devastating finality. Yet, I was reminded recently through the words of Steve

Mitchell as he led worship that God has another side, which is very tender and emotional. He is truly hurt by our rebellion and disobedience to Him and His Word. Impurity brings great pain to the heart of God because He takes it personally. We, in the same way, should take our call to purity with great sobriety.

UNDERVALUING PURITY

The sensitive side of God is described well in the Song of Solomon. His heart is ravished through one receptive glance from our eyes: "You have ravished my heart, my sister, my bride; you have ravished my heart with a glance of your eyes, with one jewel of your necklace" (Song of Solomon 4:9 NRSV). Imagine how a life full of loving obedience could develop the intimate romance Jesus desires to have with each one of us as part of His bride. Each move we make toward the Lover of our souls strengthens the shared bond of love. Every time we say yes to Him, His tender heart is ravished again and again.

If we continue to live in impurity, God's passionate love for us does not change; however, the intimate connectedness of our relationship with Him will not remain the same. This is not a vengeful response on God's part, but the natural result of our thoughts and actions which persist in opposition to His holiness. God is completely holy and if we are to be in Him and He is to be in us, as Jesus declared (John 17:21), we must honestly pursue holiness. Without holiness, the writer of Hebrews says, "No one will see the Lord" (12:14) and Jesus said something very similar when He said a pure heart was a prerequisite to seeing God: "Blessed are the pure in heart, for they will see God" (Matthew 5:8).

By one sacrifice on the cross Jesus has made all who are saved positionally perfect as He continues to make them holy in all their conduct: "Because by one sacrifice he has made perfect forever those who are being made holy" (Hebrews 10:14). We are led into holiness through the presence of the Holy Spirit within us. The Spirit puts God's laws into our hearts and writes them in our minds: "This is the covenant I will make with them after that time, says the Lord. I will put my laws in their hearts, and I will write them on their minds" (Hebrews 10:16). The indwelling Spirit of God shows us the way we should go just as He led the Israelites with the cloud by day and the fire by night (Deuteronomy 1:33). Following the leading of the Spirit is not difficult, as is often thought to be the case. The glory of God passing before us makes the way of the righteous level and smooth (Isaiah 26:7). When we are faithful with a small degree of God's intimate presence, He gives us more – similar to what was done in the parable of the talents (Matthew 25:28-29). As we continue to increase in our connectedness with God through the Holy Spirit, we are literally and permanently changed.

THE CYCLE OF PURITY

We have a tendency to undervalue the importance of purity and overestimate the difficulty in achieving it. Purity is worthy of passionate pursuit by all believers. We cannot become holy with our own effort – holiness can only be achieved by the Spirit of God producing fruit in our lives. Yet when our bodies are earthly temples which house the actual presence of God's Holy Spirit, we are effortlessly drawn into living lives that are holy. God's glory transforms us to become more and more holy because that is His nature. It is truly a joy to become pure before the Lord. We demonstrate how much we value God's free gift of love by lovingly returning it to Him through faithful obedience. Jesus said, "If anyone loves me, he will obey my teaching. My Father will love him, and we will come to him and make our home with him" (John 14:23).

God's plan for purity is extremely simple, yet wise and effective. Because God is love (1 John 4:8), we receive His love through experiencing His presence. God's love and His presence are permanently linked together. We respond to God's love by loving Him in return. "We love because he first loved us," John writes (1 John 4:19). And as Jesus said in John 14, we demonstrate our love for God by voluntary obedience. When we lovingly obey the One who calls us to be holy (Leviticus 11:45), God actually changes us to become more like Himself. What occurs is not theology or semantics. Through transformation by God we literally become more pure in our hearts and holy in His sight.

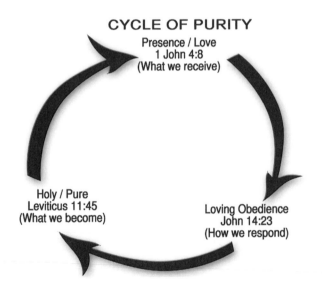

CYCLE OF PURITY

Presence / Love
1 John 4:8
(What we receive)

Holy / Pure
Leviticus 11:45
(What we become)

Loving Obedience
John 14:23
(How we respond)

This cycle of purity can become self-perpetuating and never ending. Like a snowball on a mountainside, it gains momentum and continually builds upon itself. As we become holy, God will more freely share His presence with us. We respond to the increase in His loving presence with more consistent willful obedience. When we are more faithful to God's leading, He increases our level of purity. We literally become holy to the Lord and an attractive resting place for the manifest glory of Holy God. The importance of this eternally revolving cycle cannot be overstated. If we are to fulfill the purpose for which we were created, it is essential that we become holy and reflect His character in our lives.

PURITY FOR OUR ENTIRE LIFE

Purity before God is regularly taught to young men and women during their courtship years, and unfortunately, this teaching is often ignored when it comes to actual practice. Participation in sexual sin at any age results in harmful ripples that cause a degree of personal and relational injury which can persist throughout life. There is good reason Paul instructs us that even a hint of impurity is improper for God's holy people: "But among you there must not be even a hint of sexual immorality, or of any kind of impurity ... because these are improper for God's holy people" (Ephesians 5:3). He also writes to the church in Corinth with the warning, "Flee from sexual immorality" (1 Corinthians 6:18). These are strong words due to the extreme damage caused by every sexual relationship outside of marriage. Certainly, God's grace is sufficient to limit the harm that is done when people participate in these sins, and we must remember that there is "no condemnation for those who are in Christ Jesus" (Romans 8:1). Still, as David learned after his sin with Bathsheba, participation with sin causes serious injury to those involved, and it results in far reaching negative consequences (2 Samuel 12:9-14).

Although we tend to relax our attention to this matter after marriage vows are taken, the importance of complete purity does not decrease in the least. The convenience and availability of sexual gratification with a marital partner does not alter patterns of self-centeredness, rebellion, and lust, which may have been present for years before the wedding. If Satan has been successful in draw-ing a couple into sinful behavior prior to marriage, it is certain his efforts to destroy their lives will not stop simply because mari-tal vows have been spoken, even when spoken with real commit-ment.

Sexual purity in marriage is much more than avoiding the phys-ical act of adultery. Our sexual interest must be completely directed towards our own spouse if we are to walk in righteousness and holi-ness before the Lord. This focus is achieved only by submitting full control of our thoughts, plans, recreational activities, entertain-ment options, and relationships to the Holy Spirit. Our imagina-tions must also be completely under the lordship of Jesus. Even during sexual relations within marriage, our imaginations can drift into impurity and wickedness. Any form of persistent impurity can destroy close connectedness with God and eventually devastate the physical and emotional intimacies so vital to marriage.

Source of Hope

Recognition of sinful behavior can actually be a source of hope. Our desire to become more holy can be renewed by the realization that we have not yet reached perfection. The confession of our sins to others, often including our spouses, is required if God is to for-give our sins and purify us from all unrighteousness. John wrote, "If we claim to be without sin, we deceive ourselves and the truth is not in us. If we confess our sins, he is faithful and just and will forgive us our sins and purify us from all unrighteousness" (1 John 1:8-9). The supernatural love of God can draw us into faithful obe-dience, honoring His complete lordship over our lives.

After being confronted by Nathan the prophet, David confessed his sin and humbled himself before God (2 Samuel 12:16). He again walked in obedience before the Lord, fulfilling the ultimate destiny for which he was created. Regardless of what we have done, God is quite capable of transforming us into the holy priests we were created to be (1 Peter 2:5). David's whole destiny wasn't thwarted because he fell in a moment of weakness. No, God still used all things together for good to fulfill His purpose in David's life, even extending blessing through David's descendants to us today.

GOD'S PERFECT PLAN

As holy priests of a Holy God, we are called to do our part in accomplishing the plan of holy matrimony. Within each of us is immense capability to receive and give supernatural love. Solomon compares marital relationships, as well as our relationships with God, to a magnificent garden filled with every imaginable visual, tactile, and olfactory pleasure.

Solomon wrote:

You are a garden locked up, my sister, my bride; you are a spring enclosed, a sealed fountain. Your plants are an orchard of pomegranates with choice fruits, with henna and nard, nard and saffron, calamus and cinnamon, with every kind of incense tree, with myrrh and aloes and all the finest spices. You are a garden fountain, a well of flowing water streaming down from Lebanon. – Song of Solomon 4:12-15

In God's perfect plan, both men and women enter marriage as virgins. Purity at this point in life is compared to a locked garden, an enclosed spring, and a sealed fountain. The potential for growth, pleasure, and the creation of life is contained for years, held back for its celebratory release at the consummation of marriage. In marriage we are set free to enjoy complete relational and sexual pleasure when two are united by God to become one flesh.

The garden fountain and the well of flowing water of verse 15 represent the streams of living water Jesus said would flow out of us (John 7:38). A believing spouse brings this same living water to the garden of marriage. In supernatural marriage the literal presence of the true and living God is carried within the marital relationship. The life-giving water of the Spirit springs forth forever from the perfect love of God. With a never-ending supply of life pouring into the garden, its potential for growth is limitless. The water streaming down from Lebanon into Israel was delightfully unpolluted. Similarly, every spouse in intimate communion with God brings into the relationship pure "water welling up to eternal life" (John 4:14). This garden is gloriously beautiful because it is constantly supplied with pure water for vitality and growth.

Supernatural marriage is much like the magnificent garden described in the Song of Solomon. When both partners earnestly pursue intimacy with God and with each other, their relationship can be filled with astounding beauty through the continual presence of God Himself. When they are in God and God is in them, their marital garden becomes a modern reiteration of the idyllic oneness enjoyed by Adam and Eve in the Garden of Eden. If both spouses truly seek first the Kingdom of God and His righteousness, all the things that are needed for their life and ministry together will be given to them as well (Matthew 6:33).

WE HAVE ALL SINNED

Akin to Adam, we "all have sinned and fall short of the glory of God" (Romans 3:23). Any form of disobedience will temporarily block our full participation in the joy set before us. When we become aware of imperfection, we must not become discouraged. We can continue to be thankful because boundless opportunities still remain.

God's angel shouted to Lot as he and his family fled for their lives from the evil of Sodom and Gomorrah: "Flee for your lives! Don't look back, and don't stop anywhere in the plain! Flee to the mountains or you will be swept away!" (Genesis 19:17). As we flee we must not look back in any way to the evil of our past experiences. Our freedom will be endangered by either reliving the pleasures of sin or holding on to shame related to our rebellion against God. It is equally important to not rest and become content with where we are or the level of holiness we have achieved. The risk of spiritual death is very real if we rest in the plain of self-satisfaction. All of us need to become more holy before the Lord, and none of us have attained perfect holiness in this life. This goal will only be approached if we continue our flight up the mountain towards God's dwelling place. The path to increased purity is through pursuing and abiding in the presence of Holy God.

Linda and I have been far from perfect, yet we have been allowed to experience joys beyond our expectations throughout our marriage. There were years I rested in the plain, believing that relaxation was acceptable because I was already near the top of the mountain. Considering that portion of my life, I can clearly see that during those years little of eternal value was experienced by me or accomplished through me. But God is faithful even when we are not. Although we are weak vessels, God's all-surpassing power can still be shown through us (2 Corinthians 4:7).

Three years ago, to my great surprise, God supernaturally opened my eyes and permitted me to see a glimpse of His glory. The Lord allowed me to taste and see that He is indescribably good. Since then I have recognized that the beauty of God's supernatural marital garden is beyond human imagination. The delight of enjoying its fruit cannot be exaggerated or even adequately described using words. God, through His undying love and matchless wisdom, has repaid me for the years the locusts destroyed (Joel 2:25). We truly "are more than conquerors through" the power and glory of "him who loved us" (Romans 8:37). His promises are just as real for you as they are for me. There is no reason to accept defeat when, as overcomers, we are led into triumph by the conquering "King of kings and Lord of lords" (1 Timothy 6:15).

Relationship Full of Passion

The love relationship we have with God is intended to be full of passion. He desires for His love to burn within us like blazing fire and hold on to us as tenaciously as a grave embraces mortal bodies in death. Solomon again wrote: "Place me like a seal over your heart, like a seal on your arm; for love is as strong as death, its jealousy unyielding as the grave. It burns like blazing fire, like a mighty flame" (Song of Solomon 8:6). God designed the love between partners in marriage to run parallel to our love relationship with Him. We are supernaturally drawn to our lifelong lovers by an unrelenting, fiery passion to be one with them while on earth as we will forever be one with God Himself.

There are many ways this relational zeal can be expressed and received. Certainly sexual intimacy is a wonderful means of demonstrating passionate love. There are times, however, when this kind of physical closeness is not an option. Still, the communication of fervent love should remain. Passion needs to be shared between marriage partners even in the absence of sexual relations. During these times romantic feelings, consistent commitment, and intense love can continue to be shared between spouses in many verbal and non-verbal ways. Creativity becomes even more important when the number of options is reduced.

True purity is required of both partners in marriage if their relationship is to be consistently satisfying and healthy. In my opinion, nothing has more potential to damage or destroy marital unity than unfaithfulness – whether it is unfaithfulness in word, thought, or action. Spouses who exhibit complete faithfulness to their partners establish an environment of trust, which is fertile soil for the growth of genuine love and joyful romance. It is also an environment of trust where there is growth in satisfying sexual intimacy.

SEXUALITY IS A GIFT FROM GOD

Human sexuality is a divine gift from the Giver of all that is needed and of everything that is good. When it is experienced within the perfectly safe boundaries of the marriage bed it becomes one of the means by which God grants to His loved children indescribable peace of body, soul, and spirit. This transcends all understanding (Philippians 4:7). The primary method of receiving the gift of peace is direct and intimate Spirit to spirit connectedness with Jesus, the Prince of Peace. However, when married believers, each filled with the Spirit of Jesus, come together as one flesh, their union touches both the natural and supernatural realms. The result can be a time of complete oneness between man, woman, and God – a moment of epiphany which sends ripples of great significance through both the temporal and eternal spheres.

Sexual intimacy within marriage is the adult version of the kindergarten playground I wrote about in the first chapter. The point of that story was that the boundaries God has established are not at all meant to restrict our pleasure in life. Rather, they protect us and bless us by enabling husband and wife to fully enjoy every reasonable and safe form of physical interaction.

The Holy Spirit is directly in the center of supernatural marriage. Where "the Spirit of the Lord is, there is freedom" (2 Corinthians 3:17). Within the holy covenant of marriage we are completely free to live and to love. Sex is designed by God to be incredibly enjoyable and satisfying to both husband and wife. Through marriage we are free to pursue it, explore it, and enjoy it. As God reveals to us how to fully give and receive love with one another, we become free indeed.

God's plan for us is totally perfect. When we obediently and willingly respond to His leading, we are blessed beyond our wildest dreams in every area of our lives. The phrase Linda heard while swimming that day in the YMCA pool is simple, yet profound. For those involved in supernatural marriage it is dependably true. Holy really is FUN! Now, get out there and enjoy that playground!

Conclusion

Supernatural marriage is neither the impossible dream nor an unreachable star. It is not reserved for the fortunate few, but is the attainable destiny of all whom God calls into holy matrimony. This type of marital relationship is not only available for someone else. It is available for you.

Supernatural marriage is not suddenly experienced at once in its complete fullness. The only way to get there is to start where we are and begin moving towards the goal, which is where God has planned for us to be. The Holy Spirit will lead us every step of the way in this pursuit, with the result of intimate connectedness beyond understanding and blessings beyond measure.

My hope is that those reading this book will dramatically raise their level of expectation concerning what marriage can and should be. God wants us to experience and share everything that is available in the glorious Kingdom of light. He never calls His people to accept compromise or pursue mediocrity. Because it is nearly impossible to progress beyond our goals, it is vital that they be set extremely high.

Supernatural marriage prophetically points to the ultimate oneness we will experience as believers when we, as the bride of Christ, are forever united with Jesus the Bridegroom. It is appropriate that we aim for perfection in the way we relate to our earthly spouses as we are prepared to enter a completely flawless relationship with Jesus in heaven.

The revelation shared in the writing of this book is not intended only for those who live within the geographical limits of North America. Its application is not restricted to marital partners in regions dominated by the thought patterns of western civilization. Cultural variations do not alter the eternal truths of God and His Word. His presence, passion, and power are available to every spouse in every nation on earth. God's plan for marriage is just as perfect in Beijing as it is in Auckland, Nairobi, Santiago, Dallas, or Berlin.

The universal applicability of the principles of supernatural marriage was brought to my attention at the close of a conference Linda and I led in Africa. Isaac, one of the participants, came to me at the close of the final session and spoke these words that still resound within my memory today: "What you taught challenged me and changed the way I think. When I return home, I will use the things I learned to change my church and change my country." It is my prayer that *Supernatural Marriage* will propel marital unions throughout the world toward fulfilling the destinies God has placed before them.

Two years ago I received an unforgettable dream. In the dream was a wooden treasure chest which could not be opened with any ordinary key. A special wooden key was placed in my right hand that easily unlocked the lid. When opened, a red liquid poured out of the chest and quickly spread to cover the entire earth. Everything the liquid touched was immediately transformed from apparent death to vivid and colorful life.

I am confident that a significant part of my personal destiny is to release the treasure of supernatural marriage into the Kingdom of God on earth. Satan has done too much to bring death and destruction to our world by perverting God's glorious plan for marriage. Divinely revealed truth can rapidly transform relationships filled with impending death to marriages overflowing with abundant life.

Remember this: "But seek first his kingdom and his righteousness, and all these things will be given to you as well" (Matthew 6:33). We will only receive the full blessings of the covenant of marriage as we make seeking the Kingdom of God our first priority. Intimately knowing God draws us naturally into a righteous life that demonstrates the lordship of Jesus. Only when Jesus is Lord will the Father reveal to us the mysteries of His Kingdom and share with us secrets of the ages. "The Lord confides in those who fear him; he makes his covenant known to them" (Psalm 25:14).

Now is the time for us as believers to discover the joy and beauty only found in truly holy matrimony. Supernatural marriage is one of the hidden treasures in the Kingdom of God (Matthew 13:44). Its mysteries are hidden in such a way that only those who diligently seek Him will be rewarded by their joyful discovery. Supernatural marriage is a secret treasure of the Lord being revealed to the people of God today. May it belong "to us and our children forever" (Deuteronomy 29:29).

ADVICE TO LAURA:

HOW TO LIVE WHEN UNEQUALLY YOKED

*L*inda and I recently spent an evening talking and praying with a woman who I will call Laura for the purpose of protecting her identity. For years she has been committed to obediently following Jesus with her whole heart. Her faith in God is real and her love for Him is deep. Laura is a serious and mature believer.

The primary frustration in Laura's life is that her husband is a nominal Christian who is quite content to stay the way he is. He likes to be with Laura and resents the time she spends away from him while participating in worship, Bible study, prayer, and being involved in certain aspects of ministry. The most important and enjoyable part of Laura's life is the time she spends closely connecting with God. Yet she cannot talk about this with her husband because doing so leaves him angry and even annoyed.

Long ago the powers of darkness erected a spiritual wall between Laura and her husband. These two individuals are one flesh in marriage, but they see life from the perspectives of two different kingdoms. Laura and her husband hold diverging beliefs as to what is ultimately of true value in their lives. With time the wall between them has become so thick that it seems impenetrable to the sharing of healthy emotions or the communication of love.

Laura had become extremely discouraged and was at risk of losing all hope for the future of her marriage. Neither she nor her husband lacked commitment to the relationship, they had no desire to separate, and their love for each other was unquestionably real. Yet neither of them were satisfied with the quality of their marital relationship. Things between them had been slightly off balance for years and there was no hint that improvement would be coming anytime soon.

Laura came to visit with Linda and me about her marital struggles. She did not come to us asking for our wise human counsel, but seeking divine revelation along with us. Only the supernatural wisdom of a holy God can provide solutions to seemingly insurmountable problems. The received presence of the Holy Spirit in even one partner gives the marital union access to the miraculous assets of God's Kingdom of light. Supported by the glory of the Lord, the improbable becomes probable and the impossible becomes possible.

There are many people just like Laura out there, both male and female, who experience an uncomfortable disconnect with their spouses over spiritual matters. The degree of separation caused by this is varied, but is always of significance. Even when both partners are solidly committed to God, Satan uses spiritual division as a weapon to attack individual relationships with God and undermine the stability of the marriage covenant itself. If this assault is not countered with the truth, love, and power of God, the result can be devastating.

I honor the Laura's of the world who demonstrate courage, integrity, and strength of commitment by staying the course, though unequally yoked in their marriages. Often it appears easier to simply leave, but they continue in relationship with their partners because of their desire to honor God. Hope seems barely real at times, yet it remains because they believe in God's unchanging truth and the goodness of His plan. They don't give up because they know "with God all things are possible" (Matthew 19:26).

If you are in the same situation as Laura today, allow me to remind you of a few things you already know concerning the struggles of your marriage. Sometimes it is helpful to hear truth again as if it were the very first time. God joyfully shares His wisdom and knowledge with those who desire to learn. Through God's wisdom and knowledge being communicated, He will prosper both you and your marital union. You will be blessed when you find wisdom and gain understanding, for these are more profitable than silver and yield better returns than gold (Proverbs 3:13-14). Through knowledge your life will be "filled with rare and beautiful treasures" (Proverbs 24:4). Because you have tasted the sweet goodness of God, there is "a future hope for you, and your hope will not be cut off" (Proverbs 24:14).

> For the Lord gives wisdom, and from his mouth come knowledge and understanding. He holds victory in store for the upright, he is a shield to those whose walk is blameless, for he guards the course of the just and protects the way of his faithful ones.   – Proverbs 2:6-8

Practical Tips

Following are a few of the things God brought to our minds the night we talked and prayed with Laura:

- Just like you, your spouse was created in God's image. There are abilities and attributes placed in them which are part of God's sovereign will. These things are worthy of respect. So, honor your spouse whenever this is appropriate.

- Let the peace of Christ rule in your heart and be thankful (Colossians 3:15). Honestly express thankfulness whenever possible for your spouse and for the things they do.

- God has a wonderful plan for you, and He has a specific and amazing plan for your marital partner as well.

- Jesus loved your spouse enough to die for them.

- You must learn to supernaturally love (agape) your mate even if this does not appear to be deserved in the natural realm. Jesus said to even "love your enemies" (Matthew 5:44).

- Your loving behavior must not be dependent on your partner's response. Jesus loved us first while we were totally undeserving. He died for us knowing we would behave in ungodly ways (Romans 5:6). "We love because he first loved us" (1 John 4:19).

- The kind of love required cannot come from within you or be manufactured by your will. Ask for revelation as to how to love your spouse. Supernatural love for another person is not based on who they are now. It is enabled by prophetically visualizing who that person was created to be.

- Accept and obey creative instructions from the Holy Spirit as to how to show love to your partner. Do not reject anything you are told to do by the Spirit of God. The ways of God often do not make sense to our natural minds, but

when we are obedient, they always produce wonderful results.

- Do not compromise by accepting a mediocre result. Continue to pursue every aspect of supernatural marriage available to you and your spouse.

- Do not be discouraged by your present circumstances.
  Where you are today does not limit where God can take
  you in the future.

- Miraculous transformation can happen in a moment. So
  be expecting the impossible to happen at any moment.

- Hope will not disappoint you (Romans 5:5). God placed
  hope in your heart to give you the joy, strength, and faithfulness that bridge across Satan's trap of discouragement.
  Do not underestimate the significance of your role in completing God's plan. The fulfillment of hope is catalyzed by
  the supernatural love of God flowing through you. This
  unstoppable love will bless you and your entire household.

- Do not place blame on the spouse to whom you are unequally yoked. Blame will breed bitterness and resentment.
  This further injures a relationship instead of fostering healing.

- There is never an acceptable excuse for words or actions
  intended to cause pain. Inappropriate things said or done
  by your partner do not justify retaliation. We are instructed
  to bless even those who persecute us: "Bless those who persecute you; bless and do not curse" (Romans 12:14).

- 2 Timothy 2:23-24 instructs us, "Don't have anything to
  do with foolish and stupid arguments, because you know

they produce quarrels. And the Lord's servant must not quarrel; instead, he must be kind to everyone." Everyone includes your marital partner. Arguments cannot continue if the fruit of the Spirit is supernaturally present in your heart and mind, and expressed in your words. Ask God for more of the fruit of the Spirit to be produced and evident in your life.

- Avoid dwelling on critical thoughts of your spouse. These bring further harm to an already unhealthy relationship. Take every thought captive to obey Christ (2 Corinthians 10:5). "Whatever is noble" and "whatever is admirable ... think about such things" (Philippians 4:8).

- How big is your God? Giving up hope indicates a belief that your marital relationship is too crippled for even God to heal. Do you really believe His promises? Trust that God will provide everything you need to live out your life (2 Peter 1:3).

- Earnestly ask God for help. Then, do everything He shows you to do with the wisdom, patience, kindness, and goodness He supplies. Consistently demonstrate all fruit of the Spirit. This is not only your job description; it is who you are meant to be.

- Regardless of your partner's responses, righteous living is not in vain. Godly behavior will store up treasures in heaven for you (Matthew 6:20) and can sanctify an unbelieving spouse (1 Corinthians 7:14).

- Jesus came that you could have life to the full (John 10:10). Abundant life in you attracts your spouse to the Source of life.

KEY TO ABUNDANT LIFE

The key to abundant life is true intimacy with God. The more deeply you are in love with Him, the more genuinely you can love your spouse. God's perfect love is ultimately the source of everything required to create and sustain supernatural marriage. You must not lose hope, because nothing can separate you from this everlasting love (Romans 8:35). Ultimately, His love is all you need.

Laura, your desire for supernatural marriage is not a selfish wish. It is a spiritual recognition of how things should be. You may be confident His plan for you is completely good (Jeremiah 29:11). God's Word is truth (John 17:17) and every one of His promises will be fulfilled (Joshua 23:14). I pray that you will be blessed as you read the words of this passage from Isaiah 61. God wrote them for you. Indeed, they were written about you...

> The Spirit of the Sovereign Lord is on me, because the Lord has anointed me to preach good news to the poor. He has sent me to **bind up the brokenhearted**, to proclaim **freedom** for the captives and **release** from darkness for the prisoners, to proclaim the year of the Lord's favor and the day of vengeance of our God, to **comfort all who mourn**, and **provide for those who grieve** in Zion – to bestow on them a crown of **beauty instead of ashes**, the oil of **gladness instead of mourning**, and a **garment of praise instead of a spirit of despair**. They will be called **oaks of righteousness, a planting of the Lord for the display of his splendor.**
>
> They will **rebuild** the ancient ruins and **restore the places long devastated**; they will **renew the ruined** cities that have been devastated for generations. Aliens will shepherd your flocks; foreigners will work your fields and vineyards. And you will be called **priests of the Lord**, you will be named

ministers of our God. You will feed on the wealth of nations, and in their riches you will boast.

Instead of their shame my people will receive a double portion, and instead of disgrace they will rejoice in their inheritance; and so they will inherit a double portion in their land, and everlasting joy will be theirs.

– Isaiah 61:1-7

QUESTIONS FOR STUDY, DISCUSSION, AND REFLECTION

we can do this 2gether if u want 😉

Chapter 1 – Holy Is Fun!

1. Did it initially surprise you to read that holy is fun? Where would the idea have come from that holiness prevents us from experiencing the most fun things in life? Who created the fun things in life?

2. Which fruit of the Spirit are most evident in the way you and your spouse relate to each other? Is any fruit lacking in your relationship?

Chapter 2 – The Tension of Two Realms

1. Do you have talents that need to be connected to the supernatural glory of God? Are you willing to give up personal control of your talents to the One who gave them to you?

2. How have you experienced the supernatural in your marriage?

Chapter 3 – Longing for Springtime

1. What have been the three biggest breakthroughs you have experienced in life? How did God prepare you for each one?

2. Song of Solomon 2:11-12 (TLB) says "for the winter is past ...Yes, spring is here." Which characteristics in your life would you consider winter? How might you get past these?

Chapter 4 – Texas Ablaze: Our Journey into Supernatural Encounters with God

1. How is passionate hope different from a desperate and frantic wish? Why does God honor the former more consistently than the latter?

2. What have you and your spouse done to pursue spiritual encounters with God?

Chapter 5 – You Can't Get There from Here

1. In what setting are you most apt to recognize and experience God's presence? Do you regularly place yourself in this situation? Do you think God likes being pursued?

2. "Any believer who is asking and hopeful can be filled with the Holy Spirit, who ushers us into the supernatural realm of God's Kingdom" (page 87). Do you agree or disagree with this statement? Are you and your spouse willing to ask with hope for more of God's manifest presence in your marriage?

Chapter 6 – Savior, but Lord?

1. Have you made a solid commitment to Jesus as Lord? Have you ever regretted this? Why do you think so many of us delay in truly making this commitment?

2. How does receiving God's perfect gift of love enable acceptance of lordship?

3. Read Matthew 6:33 with your spouse. Discuss areas where you are, or are not, seeking His Kingdom first.

Chapter 7 – Complete Lordship: Letting God Reign in Spirit, Soul, and Body

1. How do you react when you read in Hebrews 12:29 that "God is a consuming fire"? Does this frighten you, or are you drawn closer to Him? Why is the fire of God only good for us?

2. What effect could intimacy with God have on your ability to successfully love and bless your spouse in marriage?

3. Discuss the following statement from page 116: "Salvation is not a stagnant state of being."

Chapter 8 – The Plan of Marriage

1. Why does Satan relentlessly attack marriage? How does 1 John 4:4 give you confidence that the supernatural power of God will protect what Satan seeks to destroy?

2. What is the zeal of the Lord? How does this zeal promote supernatural marriage?

Chapter 9 – Styles of Marriage: Bitter, Tolerable, and Functional Marriage

1. When in your marriage have you trusted too much in your own wisdom and strength? How has the outcome been different when you intentionally allowed God to take control?

2. Considering 2 Corinthians 3:18, what transformation has occurred in you, in your spouse, and in the two of you together? Spend some time thanking God for the transformation He has brought about.

Chapter 10 – Styles of Marriage: Exemplary Marriage

1. Describe how all four types of love are evident in exemplary marriage: *agape, eros, storgos,* and *phileo.*

2. When has your spouse felt honored or dishonored by you? Do you regularly express words of respect to your marital partner?

3. Make a list of desires and plans your mate has surrendered out of love and honor for you. Express thankfulness to your spouse and to God today.

Chapter 11 – Styles of Marriage: Supernatural Marriage

1. Do you believe God can and will transform you to become the supernatural spouse you were created to be? Do you truly believe this can also happen to the one with whom you have become one flesh?

2. Why are both intimacy with God and submission to His lordship necessary for you to become a supernatural spouse?

3. How have you experienced God's power? Did this change the way you think about God? About life? Do you believe the power of God can improve your marriage?

Chapter 12 – The Effects of Supernatural Marriage

1. Read Matthew 18:20. What does Jesus promise whenever you and your believing spouse come together in His name?

2. What spiritual gifts might you impart to your spouse? Your partner to you?

3. Where do you see abundant life in your marital relationship? Are there areas of lack that need to be addressed?

Chapter 13 – Supernatural Romance: Emotional Intimacy

1. What are your partner's two primary love languages? Is there any godly reason to not communicate using these on a regular basis?

2. Review the practical tips for emotional intimacy on pages 218-220. Choose one or two that might be new ideas for you and enjoy implementing them in your own marriage.

Chapter 14 – Supernatural Romance: Sexual Intimacy

1. Why would God want you to become a better lover for your spouse? Does Satan want your sexual intimacy to be satisfying? Why not?

2. Discuss the following statement from page 227: "Our intimate connectedness with God continues, and is even enhanced, through pure and undefiled sexual intimacy."

Chapter 15 – The Importance of Sexual Purity

1. Purity involves our actions, thoughts, and even our imaginations. Have you recently sensed impurity in any of the three areas mentioned? Read Genesis 19:17. How can looking back with shame for past impurity be dangerous? Why is going to the mountain of God our only hope?

2. Discuss how sexual intimacy within marriage is the safe playground referred to in chapters 1 and 15.

Coming Soon!

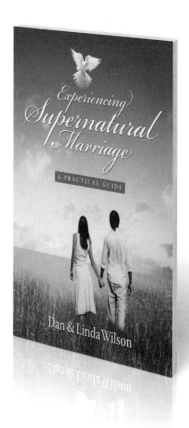

Experiencing Supernatural Marriage:
A Practical Guide

Experiencing Supernatural Marriage: A Practical Guide is designed for individuals, couples, and small groups who desire their marriages to advance further toward their planned destiny. This study guide uses statements, questions, scriptural references, and exercises to help the reader grow into deeper and more consistent relational intimacy with God and within marriage.

Dan and Linda Wilson appreciate receiving any comments you might have about *Supernatural Marriage* or their ministry. Please understand that they are not able to provide personal counsel via e-mail.

For more information concerning Supernatural Marriage Ministries, to order more copies of this book or for information about attending or hosting a Supernatural Marriage event, please visit SupernaturalMarriage.org.

You may also order more copies of *Supernatural Marriage* and other books from XP Publishing at the store at XPmedia.com

BULK ORDERS: We have bulk/wholesale prices for stores and ministries. Please contact: usaresource@xpmedia.com.

For Canadian bulk orders please contact:
resource@xpmedia.com or call 250-765-9286.

XPpublishing.com
A ministry of Christian Services Association